CHRISTMAS *Classics*

Reader's Digest
PIANO LIBRARY

50 CHRISTMAS FAVORITES ARRANGED FOR PIANO AND VOICE

Compiled by Heather Ramage
Edited by David Pearl
Cover design by Josh Labouve
Cover photograph © Comstock Images
Master recordings supplied by kind permission of Reader's Digest Music

Exclusive Distributors:
Music Sales Corporation
257 Park Avenue South, New York, NY 10010, USA
Music Sales Limited
14-15 Berners Street, London, W1T 3LJ, England
Music Sales Pty. Limited
20 Resolution Drive, Caringbah, NSW 2229, Australia.

Order No. AM993971
ISBN: 978.0.8256.3647.9

Printed in the United States of America by
Vicks Lithograph and Printing Corporation

Amsco Publications
A Part of **The Music Sales Group**
New York/London/Paris/Sydney/Copenhagen/Berlin/Tokyo/Madrid

COMPACT DISC
TRACK LISTING

Disc 1

1. Angels from the Realms of Glory (Montgomery/Smart)
Royal Philharmonic Orchestra and Chorus; Peter Knight, Conductor
2. Angels We Have Heard on High (Traditional)
Royal Philharmonic Orchestra and Chorus; Peter Knight, Conductor
3. Ave Maria (Bach/Gounod)
Jan Van Reeth, Flute & Anne Lies Sturm, Harp
4. Away in a Manger (Anonymous/Murray)
The Fireside Singers
5. The Birthday of a King (Neidlinger)
Ambrosian Singers with Organ and Chimes; John McCarthy, Conductor
6. Bring a Torch, Jeanette, Isabella (Traditional)
The Fireside Singers
7. Christmas Is Coming (Traditional)
Westminster Brass Ensemble; London Bell Ringers; John Paice, Carillon;
Leslie Pearson, Organ
8. The Coventry Carol (Traditional)
Owen Brannigan, Bass; The John McCarthy Chorus
9. Dance of the Reed Flutes from *The Nutcracker Suite* Op. 71a
(Tchaikovsky)
Slovak Radio New Philharmonic Orchestra; Shardad Rohani, Conductor
10. Dance of the Sugar Plum Fairy from *The Nutcracker Suite* Op. 71a
(Tchaikovsky)
London Promenade Orchestra; Eric Hammerstein, Conductor
11. Deck the Halls (Traditional)
Royal Philharmonic Orchestra and Chorus; Peter Knight, Conductor
12. Ding Dong! Merrily on High (Woodward/Arbeau)
David Firman, His Orchestra and Chorus
13. The First Nowell (Traditional)
Ambrosian Singers; National Philharmonic Orchestra; Charles Gerhardt, Conductor
14. Go Tell It on the Mountain (Work, Jr./African-American Spiritual)
London Festival Orchestra and Chorus
15. God Rest Ye Merry, Gentlemen (Traditional)
Richard Benson and His Orchestra
16. Good Christian Men, Rejoice (Traditional)
Ambrosian Singers with Organ and Chimes; John McCarthy, Conductor
17. Good King Wenceslas (Neale/Traditional)
The Fireside Singers
18. Hallelujah Chorus from *Messiah* (Handel)
Royal Philharmonic Orchestra and Chorus; Peter Knight, Conductor
19. Hark! The Herald Angels Sing (Wesley/Mendelssohn)
The Fireside Singers
20. The Holly and the Ivy (Traditional)
National Philharmonic Orchestra; Charles Gerhardt, Conductor
21. I Saw Three Ships (Traditional)
John McCarthy Chorus
22. In Dulci Jubilo (Traditional)
Knabenkantorei Basel; Beat Raaflaub, Conductor
23. In the Bleak Midwinter (Rossetti/Holst)
Larry Dalton, His Orchestra and Chorus
24. It Came Upon the Midnight Clear (Sears/Willis)
Beecham Choral Society; John McCarthy, Conductor; Royal Philharmonic Orchestra;
Peter Knight, Conductor
25. Jesu, Joy of Man's Desiring from *Cantata 147* (Bach)
National Philharmonic Orchestra and Chorus; Charles Gerhardt, Conductor
26. Jingle Bells (Pierpont)
National Philharmonic Orchestra; Charles Gerhardt, Conductor
27. Joseph Dearest, Joseph Mild (Traditional)
The Fireside Singers

Disc 2

1. Joy to the World (Watts/Mason)
Richmond Brass Ensemble; National Philharmonic Orchestra;
Charles Gerhardt, Conductor
2. Lo! How a Rose E'er Blooming (Traditional)
National Philharmonic Orchestra; Charles Gerhardt, Conductor
3. March of the Kings (Traditional)
The Fireside Singers
4. O Christmas Tree (Traditional)
The Fireside Singers
5. O Come, All Ye Faithful (Wade/Traditional)
Royal Philharmonic Orchestra and Chorus; Peter Knight, Conductor
6. O Come, Little Children (Schmid/Schulz)
Royal Philharmonic Orchestra and Chorus; Peter Knight, Conductor
7. O Come, O Come Emmanuel (Traditional)
Larry Dalton, His Orchestra and Chorus
8. O Holy Night (Adam)
National Philharmonic Orchestra; Charles Gerhardt, Conductor
9. O Little Town of Bethlehem (Brooks/Redner)
Gordon Langford and His Orchestra
10. O Sanctissima (Traditional)
Ambrosian Singers with Organ and Chimes; John McCarthy, Conductor
11. Once in Royal David's City (Alexander/Gauntlett)
The Mayfair Symphony Orchestra; Roderick Dunk, Conductor
12. Panis Angelicus (Franck)
John McCarthy Chorus; Leslie Fyson, Tenor; William Davies, Organ
13. Pat-A-Pan (Traditional)
The Fireside Singers
14. Silent Night (Mohr/Gruber)
Ambrosian Singers; National Philharmonic Orchestra; Charles Gerhardt, Conductor
15. The Skater's Waltz (Waldteufel)
London Promenade Orchestra; Eric Hammerstein, Conductor
16. The Sleigh Ride (L. Mozart)
Sinfonia of London; Douglas Gamley, Conductor
17. Toyland from *Babes in Toyland* (Herbert)
London Promenade Orchestra; Eric Hammerstein, Conductor
18. The Twelve Days of Christmas (Traditional)
Royal Philharmonic Orchestra and Chorus; Peter Knight, Conductor
19. The Virgin's Slumber Song (Teschemacher/Reger)
RCA Symphony Orchestra; Eric Hammerstein, Conductor
20. The Wassail Song (Traditional)
Ambrosian Singers with Organ and Chimes; John McCarthy, Conductor
21. We Three Kings of Orient Are (Hopkins)
Royal Philharmonic Orchestra and Chorus; Peter Knight, Conductor
22. We Wish You a Merry Christmas (Traditional)
National Philharmonic Orchestra with the Richmond Brass Ensemble;
Charles Gerhardt, Conductor
23. What Child Is This? (Dix/Traditional)
National Philharmonic Orchestra; Charles Gerhardt, Conductor

N.B. *Please note that the musical arrangements included in this book
may not exactly match the corresponding audio.*

TABLE OF CONTENTS

Chord Dictionary...4

About the Selections...6

Angels from the Realms of Glory (Montgomery/Smart).........12

Angels We Have Heard on High (Traditional) 14

Ave Maria (Bach/Gounod) 16

Away in a Manger (Anonymous/Murray) 24

The Birthday of a King (Neidlinger) 9

Bring a Torch, Jeanette, Isabella (Traditional) 26

Christmas Is Coming (Traditional)............................28

The Coventry Carol (Traditional) 30

Dance of the Reed Flutes from *The Nutcracker Suite* Op. 71a

   (Tchaikovsky) 32

Dance of the Sugar Plum Fairy from *The Nutcracker Suite*

   Op. 71a (Tchaikovsky) 21

Deck the Halls (Traditional) 36

Ding Dong! Merrily on High (Woodward/Arbeau) 38

The First Nowell (Traditional) 40

Go Tell It on the Mountain

   (Work, Jr./African-American Spiritual)......................46

God Rest Ye Merry, Gentlemen (Traditional) 43

Good Christian Men, Rejoice (Traditional) 48

Good King Wenceslas (Neale/Traditional)....................50

Hallelujah Chorus from *Messiah* (Handel) 52

Hark! The Herald Angels Sing (Wesley/Mendelssohn) 60

The Holly and the Ivy (Traditional) 62

I Saw Three Ships (Traditional) 64

In Dulci Jubilo (Traditional) 57

In the Bleak Midwinter (Rossetti/Holst) 66

It Came Upon the Midnight Clear (Sears/Willis).................68

Jesu, Joy of Man's Desiring from *Cantata 147* (Bach)...........70

Jingle Bells (Pierpont).......................................74

Joseph Dearest, Joseph Mild (Traditional) 77

Joy to the World (Watts/Mason) 80

Lo! How a Rose E'er Blooming (Traditional) 82

March of the Kings (Traditional)............................84

O Christmas Tree (Traditional) 86

O Come, All Ye Faithful (Wade/Traditional) 92

O Come, Little Children (Schmid/Schulz)....................94

O Come, O Come Emmanuel (Traditional) 89

O Holy Night (Adam) 96

O Little Town of Bethlehem (Brooks/Redner)..................102

O Sanctissima (Traditional) 104

Once in Royal David's City (Alexander/Gauntlett) 106

Panis Angelicus (Franck) 108

Pat-A-Pan (Traditional) 112

Silent Night (Mohr/Gruber)...............................114

The Skater's Waltz (Waldteufel)............................116

The Sleigh Ride (L. Mozart) 118

Toyland from *Babes in Toyland* (Herbert) 122

The Twelve Days of Christmas (Traditional) 124

The Virgin's Slumber Song (Teschemacher/Reger) 99

The Wassail Song (Traditional) 134

We Three Kings of Orient Are (Hopkins) 128

We Wish You a Merry Christmas (Traditional) 130

What Child Is This? (Dix/Traditional) 132

N.B. *To avoid awkward page turns the running order of this book differs slightly to that on the CDs.*

CHORD DICTIONARY

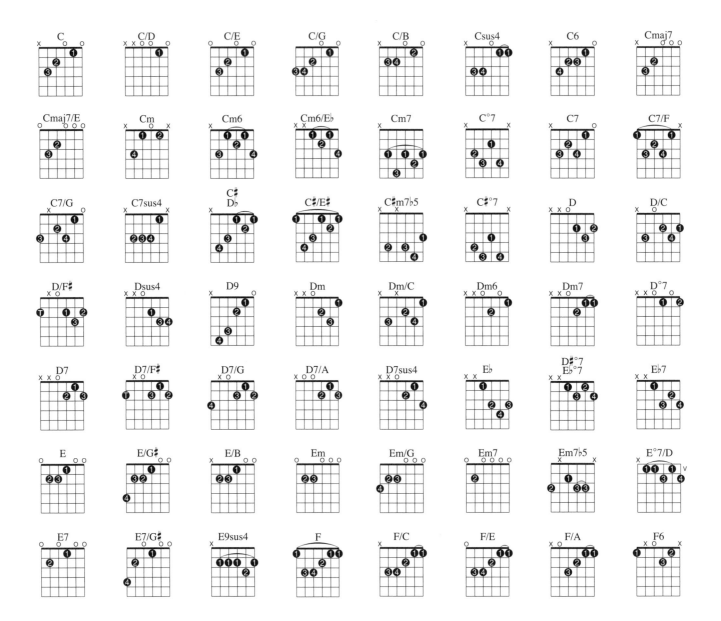

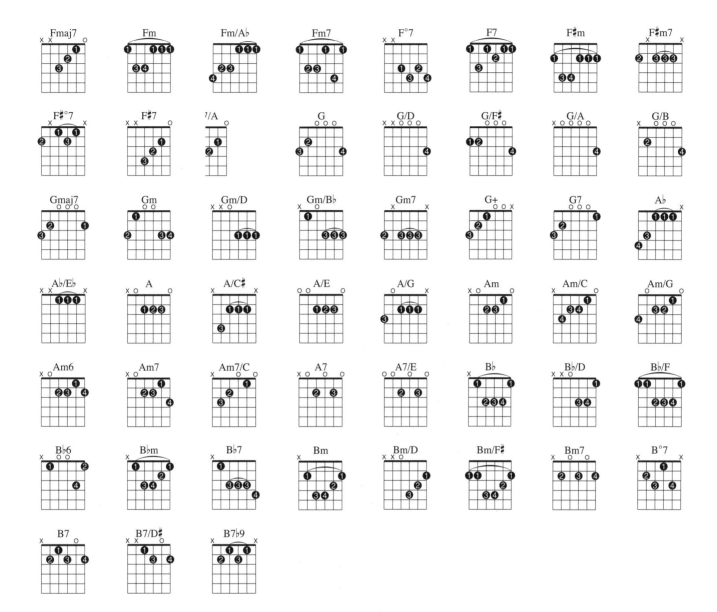

ABOUT THE SELECTIONS

No holiday has more joyous and beautiful music written for it than Christmas, and this collection brings together 50 of the best traditional carols and sacred classical works, along with great performances on CD from the vaults of Reader's Digest Music. While space is too limited to give the story behind each of the songs, this introduction attempts to illuminate the most interesting and significant among them.

Ave Maria: The Latin prayer "Ave Maria" ("Hail Mary") has been set to music by a multitude of composers, including Schubert, Mendelssohn, Mozart, Franck, Liszt, Rossini, Saint-Saëns, Verdi, and Stravinsky. The two best-known settings are by Schubert and Charles Gounod. Originally, Schubert composed his for a prayer to the Virgin Mary found in Sir Walter Scott's *The Lady of the Lake*, but later the words of the Roman Catholic prayer were substituted for Scott's. Gounod's ethereal setting itself is a hybrid, as he composed a melody over the flowing arpeggiated chords of Johann Sebastian Bach's "Prelude in C Major" from Book I of *The Well-Tempered Clavier*. It was published without words as "Méditation" in 1853, and six years later Gounod enhanced its religious nature by adding the "Ave Maria" text. The work has been recorded hundreds of times, and an early one of much historical interest can be found on **youtube.com** by the great soprano Nellie Melba (d. 1931), who was so famous that the chef Escoffier created peach melba and melba toast in her honor. (Search for: Nellie Melba Gounod Ave Maria.)

The Coventry Carol: This is one of the oldest English carols, dating back to at least 1534. It was included in a Christmas play for the Shearmen and Tailors' Guild's annual pageant on the steps of Coventry Cathedral. The play tells the story of Jesus' birth and Herod's slaughter of Jewish infants. In the play, "The Coventry Carol" is sung by a Jewish mother as a lullaby to her doomed baby son, hence its alternative title of "Lully, Lullay" (variants of "lullaby," heard in the lyrics). Musically, the carol is interesting as an example of the Picardy Third, which is the unexpected use of a major third chord at the end of a verse or section based on minor thirds.

Hallelujah Chorus from *Messiah*: George Frideric Handel wrote his greatest work, the oratorio *Messiah*, under divine inspiration in less than a month in 1741, and it was premiered in Dublin the following year. Poet Charles Jennens adapted the text from the King James Bible, mostly from chapters of Isaiah that describe the future messiah of the Jewish people. The triumphant "Hallelujah Chorus," from near the end of the work, had a tremendous affect on audiences, as it still does today.

After the success of the oratorio in Dublin, King George II attended a performance of it in London in 1743 and leapt to his feet at the opening strains of the "Hallelujah Chorus," remaining standing until the end. Of course, the rest of the audience followed suit, and thus the custom was born of standing during this section of the work.

Hark! The Herald Angels Sing: This ebullient Yuletide hymn has a distinguished pedigree. The words were written in 1739 by Charles Wesley, "the poet laureate of Methodism" and brother of its founder, John Wesley. Charles, an ordained Anglican minister before becoming a Methodist leader, wrote more than 5,000 published hymn texts, including such familiar ones as "Christ the Lord Is Risen Today," "Love Divine, All Loves Excelling," and "O for a Thousand Tongues to Sing." He was a somber, devout man who preferred that his hymns be sung to slow, dignified tunes. Still, it's hard to imagine he would have objected to the pairing of his words to a spirited melody from Felix Mendelssohn's cantata *Festgesang an die Künstler* (*Songfest for an Artist*, 1840), commemorating the 400th anniversary of Johannes Gutenberg's invention of the printing press. The credit for joining the words of "Hark! The Herald Angels Sing" to this music goes to English tenor and music teacher William H. Cummings, who had performed in Mendelssohn's oratio *Elijah* and was a fan of his choral works. Cummings's arrangement of the melody with Wesley's lyrics first appeared in the *Congregational Hymn and Tune Book* in 1857.

Jesu, Joy of Man's Desiring: Along with Mozart and Beethoven, Johann Sebastian Bach is one of the three titans of classical music. Most of his output is religious, including some 300 cantatas for church services of which about 200 survive. The cantatas typically contained chorales to be sung by a choir, interspersed with solo arias for soprano, alto, baritone, or bass voices. One of the most famous of Bach's chorales, heard frequently to this day, is "Jesu, Joy of Man's Desiring" from Cantata No. 147, entitled *Herz und Mund und Tat und Leben* (*Heart and Mouth and Deed and Life*), written in 1723. Over the stately, legato melodic line of the chorale, Bach scored a countermelody of gently swirling triplets. This angelic work is a vivid example of how much Bach was in touch with the divine when he wrote for the church. One can easily imagine it to be the music of Heaven.

Joy to the World: The "Father of English Hymnody," Isaac Watts (d. 1748), wrote the words of this most popular carol, along with some 750 other hymns, including "O God, Our

---

*Titles in **bold** are included in the songbook.*

Help in Ages Past" and "When I Survey the Wondrous Cross." The lyrics to "Joy to the World" are, in fact, a translation of Psalm 98, which Watts published in his *Psalms of David* in 1719. American religious composer Lowell Mason set them to music in 1839, saying his tune was from Handel. Although some of the musical phrases of "Joy to the World" bear resemblance to parts of Handel's *Messiah*, music historians feel that Mason, despite his generous nod to the Baroque master, deserves the lion's share of the credit as the joyous tune's creator.

Selections from *The Nutcracker Suite*: Pyotr Ilyich Tchaikovsky wrote *The Nutcracker Suite* before he had completed the entire *Nutcracker* ballet. He had been working on sections of the ballet during 1891 and remembered that he had promised to write a new work for a St. Petersburg concert in the spring of 1892. So he completed and arranged those sections into a suite of eight movements. Included here is "Dance of the Sugar Plum Fairy" and the "Dance of the Reed Flutes." The former is notable for its use of the celesta, an instrument Tchaikovsky had recently discovered in Paris. It resembled a tiny spinet piano with small silver bars instead of strings, and when struck, the bars produced a delicate bell-like sound. Both the suite and entire ballet were successes from the outset, although Tchaikovsky did not live long to enjoy it. He died in 1893 at age 53 after intentionally drinking unboiled water during a cholera outbreak, though warned not to.

O Come, All Ye Faithful: The words of this majestic carol were originally in Latin and are attributed to John Francis Wade, an Englishman who moved to a Roman Catholic community in France. It is not known whether he himself wrote the verses or found them in an old Latin text. In any event, he combined them with the music "Adeste Fideles," and the famous carol was published in the collection *Cantus Diversi* in 1751. About a century later, English clergyman Frederick Oakeley, who was interested in good literary texts to sing for congregations, made the English translation found in hymnals today. It's worth noting that the familiar recording of "O Come, All Ye Faithful" by Bing Crosby from the 1940s begins with the Latin stanzas.

O Holy Night (Cantique de Noël): French composer Adolphe Adam (d. 1856) wrote operas and ballets, the best known of which is *Giselle*. He also composed a "modest little melody," as he called it, and sent it to his friend and poet Cappeau de Roquemaure for some lyrics. The result was a powerful and immensely popular Christmas carol under the title "Cantique de Noël," although, amazingly, Roman Catholic authorities initially frowned on the song. In 1855, John Sullivan Dwight, a Unitarian minister who became America's first influential classical music critic as the founder-editor of *Dwight's Journal of Music*, adapted the verses into the English ones sung today. There is a touching story involving this carol from the Franco-Prussian War: On Christmas Eve, 1870, a French solder came out of his trench and sang "Cantique de Noël" loud enough to be heard by nearby German troops. Then a German soldier responded with a traditional German carol. For one evening at least, their guns were silent.

O Little Town of Bethlehem: Phillips Brooks was rector of Holy Trinity Church in Philadelphia when he traveled to the Holy Land in 1865. As most Christian pilgrims do, he included Bethlehem, the town of Christ's birth, on his itinerary, especially since it is a mere four miles from Jerusalem. Situated in the central mountain range of Judea, Bethlehem is surrounded by sheep pastures on hillocks separated by steep gullies. Its pastoral beauty inspired Brooks to write the verses of his carol during the Christmas season of 1868. His organist, Lewis Redner, composed the melody for their Sunday school choir, and the song soon spread among the church-going public. English carolers and American Episcopalians, however, sing the words to a different tune, "Forest Green," in an adaptation by Ralph Vaughan Williams.

Panis Angelicus: Though not written specifically with Christmas in mind, the much-performed sacred song "Panis Angelicus" by César Franck fits with the holiday's religious overtones. Franck spent most of his life as an organist in Paris, eventually at the well-known Church of St. Clotilde, where he would improvise on the organ for hours, to the amazement of admirers such as Franz Liszt and Claude Debussy. He wrote "Panis Angelicus" ("Bread of Angels") in 1872, and owing to its beautiful, flowing melodic lines, the work is often heard today. Recent recordings of it by notable sacred singers include those by Andrea Bocelli, Charlotte Church, and Michael Crawford.

Silent Night: Necessity is the mother of invention, as the saying goes, and this was certainly the case with the creation of "Silent Night," our most beloved Christmas carol. The organ in the village of Oberndorf in the Austrian Alps broke down on Christmas Eve, 1818. Pastor Josef Mohr and organist Franz Gruber needed a hymn for midnight mass that could be sung with guitar accompaniment, and they set to work with only hours to spare. "Silent Night" ("Stille Nacht" in German) was the result. It spread by word of mouth and, eventually, publication to become the most famous Christmas carol ever written.

The Skater's Waltz: Emil Waldteufel (d. 1915) was known as the "Waltz King of France" and was a favorite of Empress Eugénie, wife of Napoléon III, who had him appointed conductor of state balls. In the days before radio and TV, this was a big deal, since balls were still one of the chief entertainments of the upper classes. Waldteufel wrote hundreds of dance pieces (waltzes, polkas, galops, etc.) that were popular in his day, but the one work for which he became best known was his "Skater's Waltz" of 1882, celebrating the Parisian passion for ice skating during the winter.

Sleigh Ride: There are three pieces known as "Sleigh Ride" in the Christmas repertoire, giving rise to considerable confusion among them. The one that is most popular and heard most on the radio is Leroy Anderson's "Sleigh Ride" (1948) with lyrics by Mitchell Parish ("Just hear those sleigh bells jingling…"). However, father and son Leopold and Wolfgang Amadeus Mozart both wrote pieces called "Sleigh Ride," and that is really where the confusion sets in. Included in this volume is Leopold's, which has the proper title of "Divertimento in F Major." He composed it at least by 1756 (the year of Wolfgang's birth), since it was performed then in Augsburg, Germany. Wolfgang's "Sleigh Ride" ("Die Schlittenfahrt") is actually his "German Dance in C Major for Orchestra" (K. 605)—one of many he wrote as court composer in Vienna in 1791, during the feverish activity of his last year. Leopold's work shows the clarity and charm that were typical of his time and that he passed down to his son.

The Twelve Days of Christmas: Of indeterminate origin, this carol is quite old, probably dating from late Renaissance when counting songs were much in fashion. At that time, religious holidays were the only holidays, as they had been for centuries, and rich and poor alike preferred to extend them as much as possible. Thus, a custom arose among the wealthy of giving a gift on each of the twelve days of Christmas; that is, the twelve days between Christmas Day and Epiphany (January 6), when the Three Wise Men arrived to offer gifts and worship the Christ Child. If the less fortunate couldn't afford to give gifts on each day, at least they could sing about it.

We Wish You a Merry Christmas: This song of "good tidings we bring" is the best known of the so-called "waits' carols." In Merry Old England, "waits" were semi civil servants who were responsible for sounding fire alarms and calling out the hours of the day. At Christmas, they expanded their duties to wishing the public a hearty Merry Christmas, in hopes that they would be tipped in cash or with treats such as figgy pudding or a "cup of good cheer."

On that note, on behalf of the editors and publishers, may I raise a glass to you, our music-loving patrons, to wish you happy holidays, good health and fortune in the new year. May you also experience much joy in playing and listening to these timeless Christmas favorites.

— By Rick Hessney

The Birthday of a King

By William H. Neidlinger

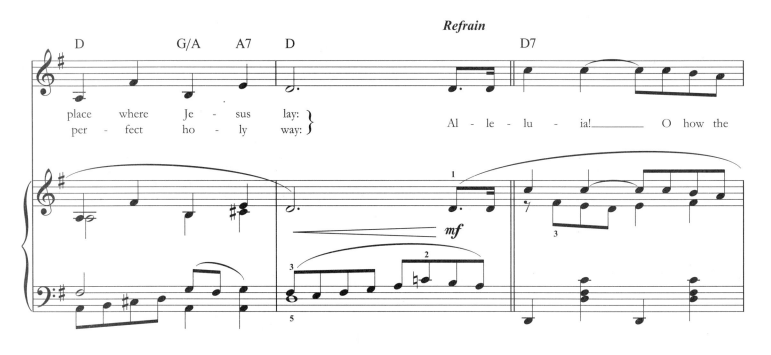

sky was bright with a ho - ly light, 'twas the birth - day of a

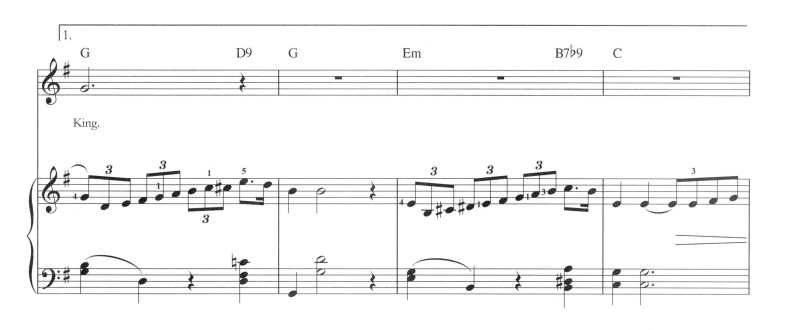

King.

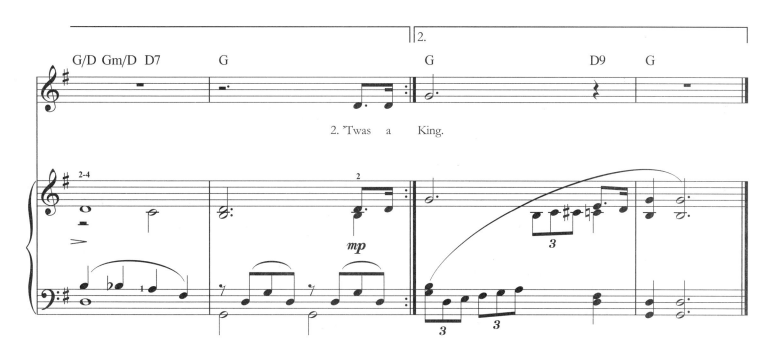

2. 'Twas a King.

Angels from the Realms of Glory

Words by James Montgomery
Music by Henry T. Smart

With Spirit

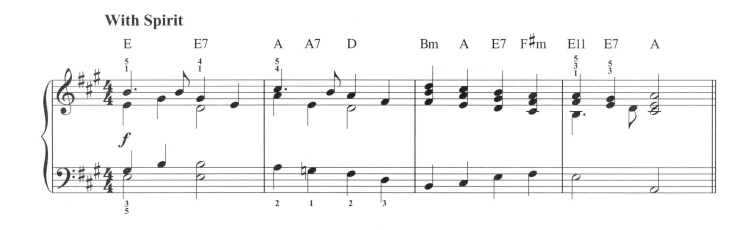

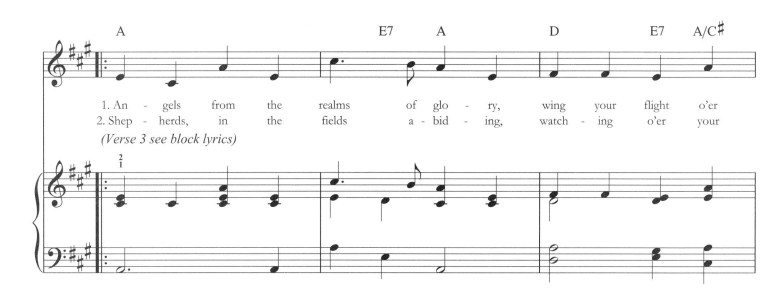

1. An - gels from the realms of glo - ry, wing your flight o'er
2. Shep - herds, in the fields a - bid - ing, watch - ing o'er your

(Verse 3 see block lyrics)

all the earth; ye who sang cre - a - tion's sto - ry,
flocks by night, God with man is now re - sid - ing,

Verse 3:
Sages, leave your contemplations,
Brighter visions beam afar;
Seek the great Desire of nations;
Ye have seen His natal star:
Refrain

Angels We Have Heard on High

Traditional French Carol

Joyously

1. An - gels we have heard on high, sweet - ly sing - ing
2. Shep - herds why this ju - bi - lee? Why your joy - ful

(Verses 3 & 4 see block lyrics)

on the plain. And the moun - tains in re - ply ech - o - ing their joy - ous strain:
strains pro - long? What the glad - some tid - ings be, which in - spire your heav' - nly song?

Verse 3:
Come to Bethlehem and see
Him whose birth the angels sing;
Come adore on bended knee
Christ, the Lord, the newborn King.
Refrain

Verse 4:
See Him in a manger laid,
Whom the choir of angels praise;
Holy Spirit lend thine aid,
While our hearts in love we raise.
Refrain

Ave Maria

By Johann Sebastian Bach and Charles Gounod

Andante con moto

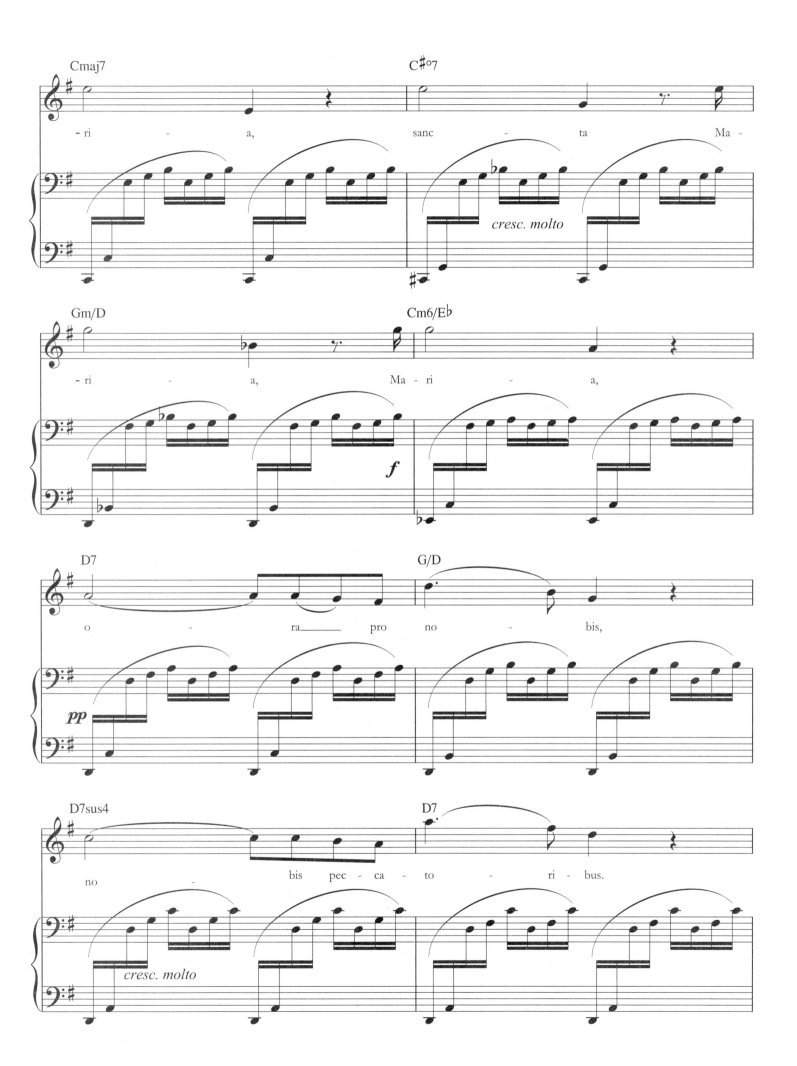

20

Dance of the Sugar Plum Fairy
from *The Nutcracker Suite* Op. 71a

By Pyotr Ilyich Tchaikovsky

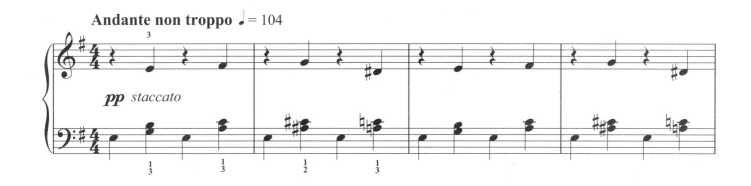

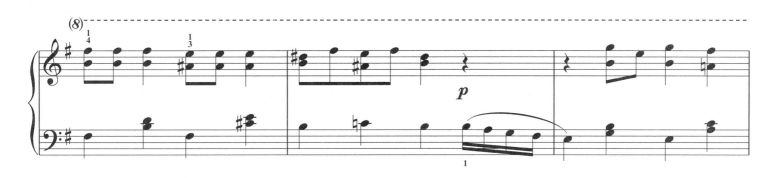

Away in a Manger

Words: Anonymous
Music by James R. Murray

Tenderly

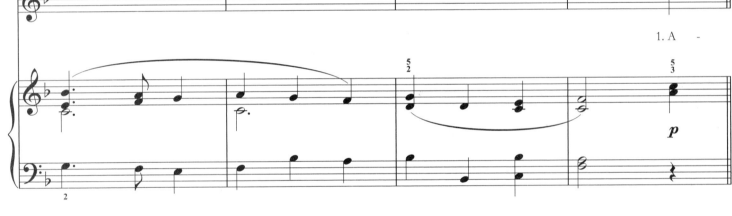

1. A -

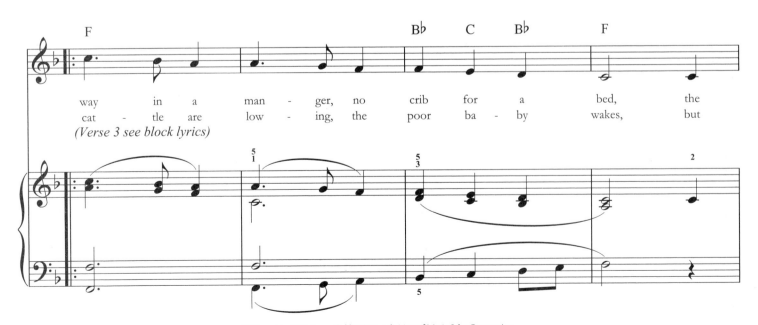

way   in   a   man - ger,   no   crib   for   a   bed,   the
cat - tle   are   low - ing,   the   poor   ba - by   wakes,   but
(Verse 3 see block lyrics)

Verse 3:

Be near me Lord Jesus, I ask thee to stay
Close by me forever and love me, I pray.
Bless all the dear children in thy tender care,
And take us to heaven to live with thee there.

Bring a Torch, Jeanette, Isabella

Traditional

The lyrics in the score:

1. Bring a torch,___ Jean-ette, Is-a-bel-la, bring a torch,___ come swift-ly and run.
2. Hast-en now,___ good folk of the vil-lage, hast-en now,___ the Christ Child to see.

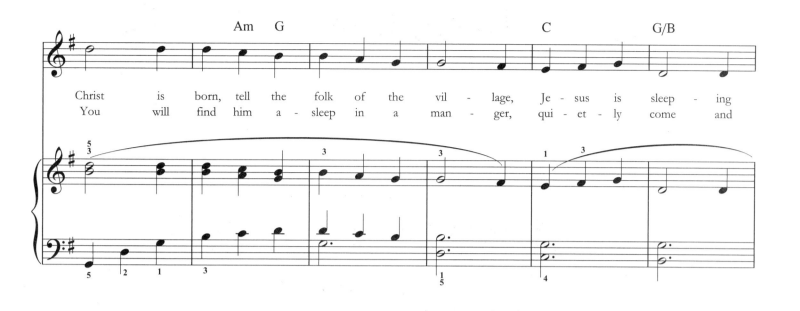

Christ is born, tell the folk of the vil - lage, Je - sus is sleep - ing
You will find him a - sleep in a man - ger, qui - et - ly come and

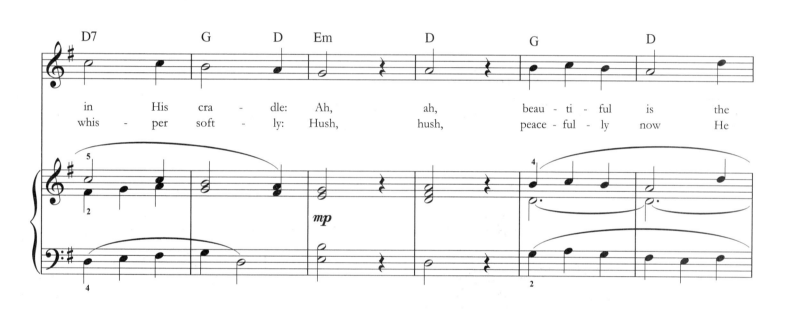

in His cra - dle: Ah, ah, beau - ti - ful is the
whis - per soft - ly: Hush, hush, peace - ful - ly now He

Moth - er. Ah, ah, beau - ti - ful is her Son.____
slum - bers. Hush, hush, peace - ful - ly now He sleeps.____

Christmas Is Coming

Traditional English Carol

Brisk March tempo

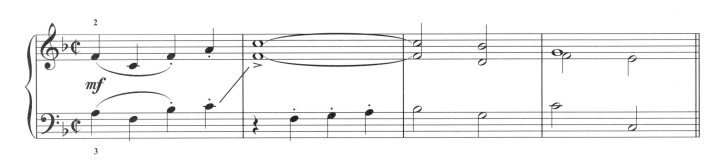

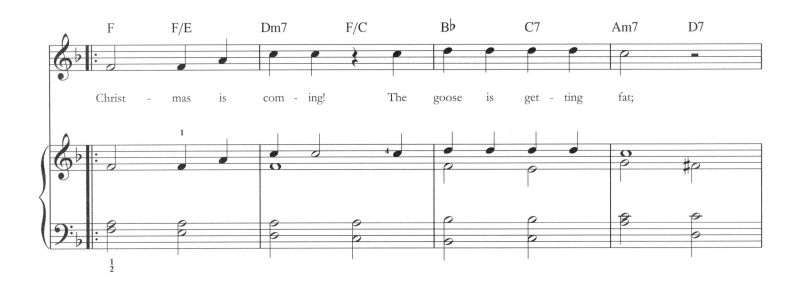

Christ - mas is com - ing! The goose is get - ting fat;

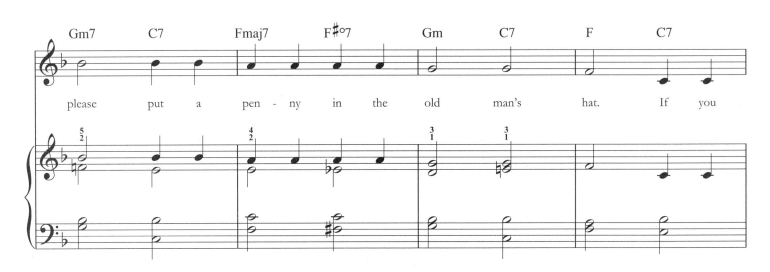

please put a pen - ny in the old man's hat. If you

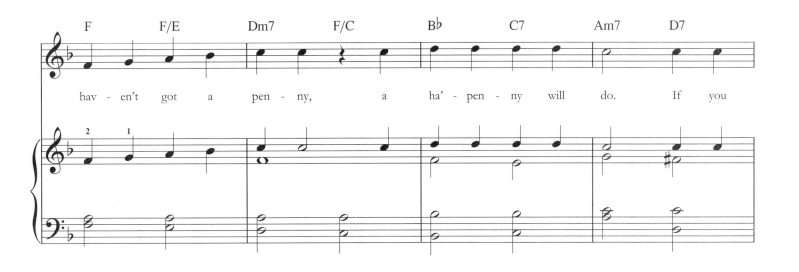

haven't got a penny, a ha'penny will do. If you

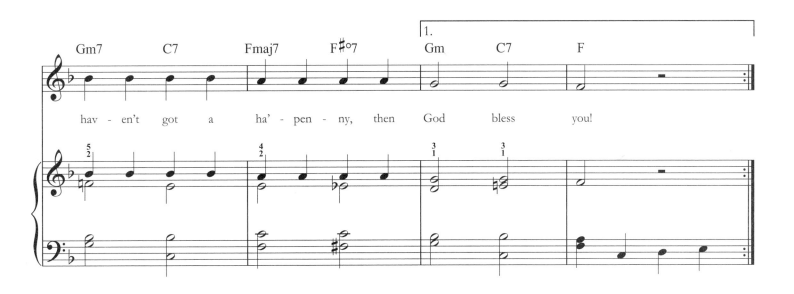

haven't got a ha'penny, then God bless you!

God bless you!

The Coventry Carol

Traditional English Carol

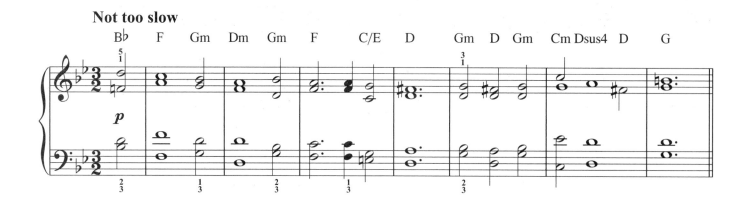

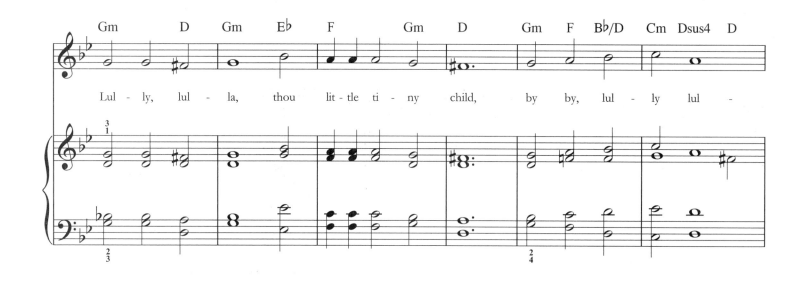

Lul - ly, lul - la, thou lit - tle ti - ny child, by by, lul - ly lul -

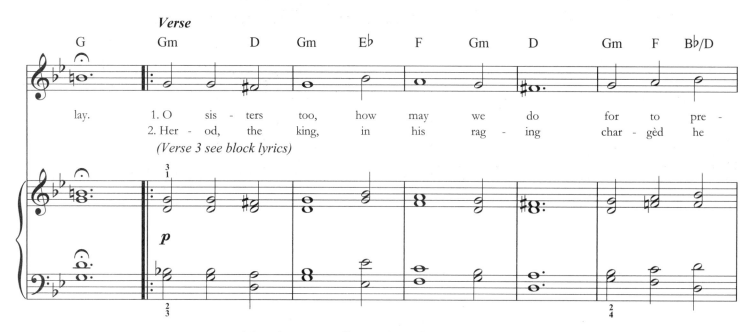

lay.

1. O sis - ters too, how may we do for to pre-
2. Her - od, the king, in his rag - ing char - gèd he

(Verse 3 see block lyrics)

Verse 3:

That woe is me, poor child for thee!
And ever morn and day.
For thy parting, neither say nor sing
By by, lully lullay!

Dance of the Reed Flutes
from *The Nutcracker Suite* Op. 71a

By Pyotr Ilyich Tchaikovsky

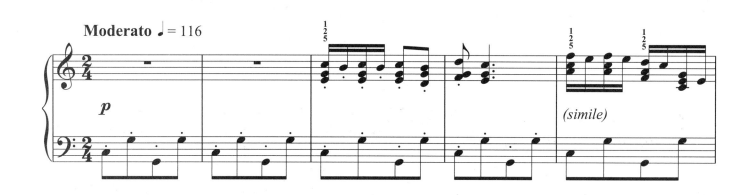

Deck the Halls

Traditional Welsh Carol

1. Deck the halls with boughs of hol - ly. Fa - la - la - la - la, la la - la - la.
2. See the blaz - ing Yule be - fore us. Fa - la - la - la - la, la la - la - la.

(Verse 3 see block lyrics)

'Tis the sea - son to be jol - ly. Fa - la - la - la la, la la - la - la.
Strike the harp and join the cho - rus. Fa - la - la - la la, la la - la - la.

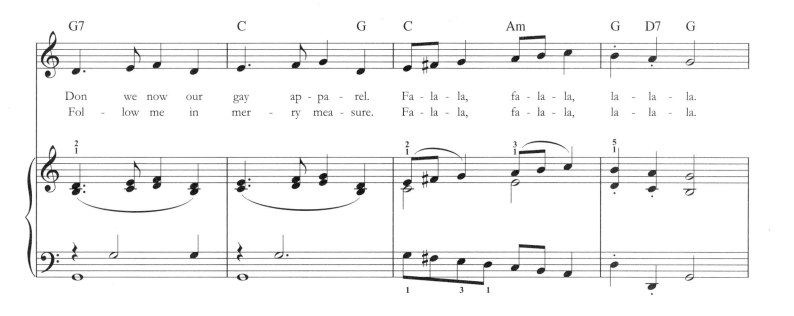

Don we now our gay ap-pa-rel. Fa-la-la, fa-la-la, la-la-la.
Fol-low me in mer-ry mea-sure. Fa-la-la, fa-la-la, la-la-la.

Troll the an-cient Yule-tide ca-rol. Fa-la-la-la la, la la-la-la.
While I tell of Yule-tide trea-sure. Fa-la-la-la la, la la-la-la.

Verse 3:

Fast away the old year passes.

Fa-la-la-la-la, la-la-la-la.

Hail the new, ye lads and lasses.

Fa-la-la-la-la, la-la-la-la.

Sing we joyous all together.

Fa-la-la, fa-la-la, la-la-la.

Heedless of the wind and weather.

Fa-la-la-la-la, la-la-la-la.

Ding Dong! Merrily on High

Words by George R. Woodward
Music by Thoinot Arbeau

Verse 3:

Pray you, dutifully prime

Your matin chime, you ringers.

May you beautifully rhyme

Your evetime song, you singers.

Refrain

The First Nowell

Traditional English Carol

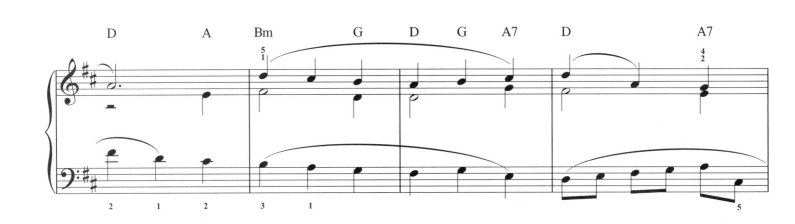

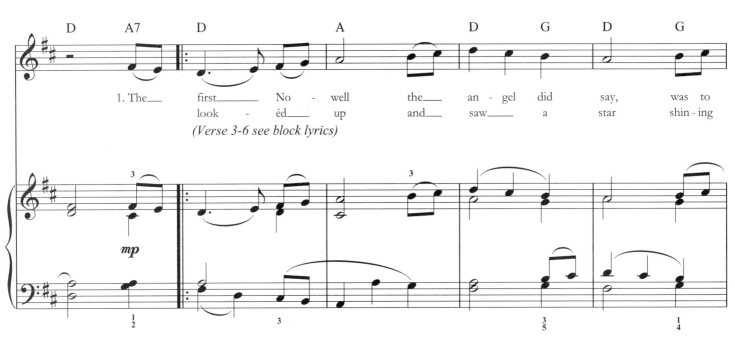

1. The____ first_____ No - well the____ an - gel did say, was to
look - éd____ up and____ saw____ a star shin - ing
(Verse 3-6 see block lyrics)

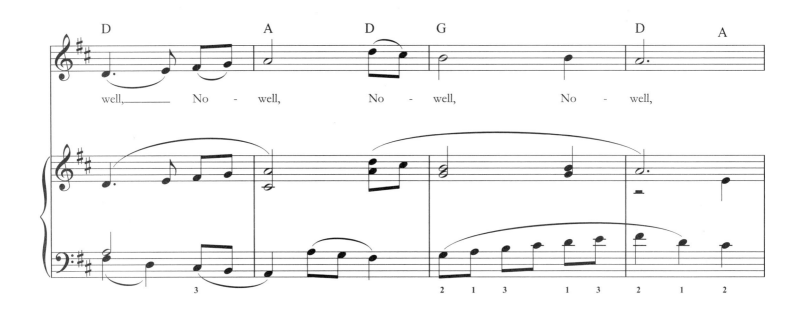

well,_____ No - well, No - well, No - well,

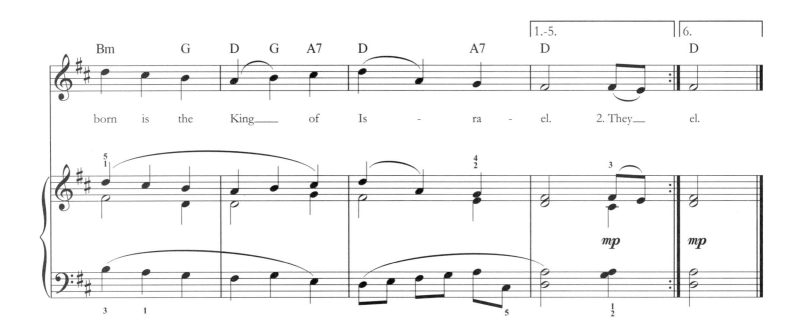

born is the King____ of Is - ra - el. 2. They___ el.

Verse 3:
And by the light of that same star,
Three Wise Men came from country far;
To seek for a King was their intent,
And to follow the star wherever it went.
Refrain

Verse 4:
This star drew nigh unto the northwest;
O'er Bethlehem it took its rest,
And there it did both stop and stay
Right over the place where Jesus lay.
Refrain

Verse 5:
Then entered in those Wise Men three,
Fell reverently upon their knee,
And offered there, in His presence,
Their gold and myrrh and frankincense.
Refrain

Verse 6:
Then let us all with one accord
Sing praises to our heavenly Lord,
That hath made heaven and earth of naught,
And with his blood mankind hath bought.
Refrain

God Rest Ye Merry, Gentlemen

Traditional English Carol

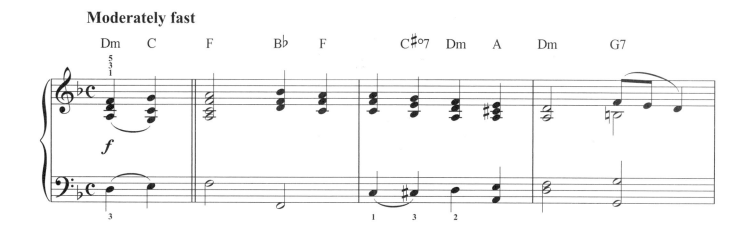

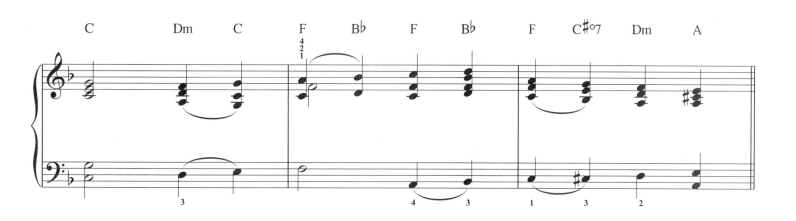

1. God rest ye mer-ry, gen-tle-men, let

God our heaven-ly Fath-er a

(Verses 3-6 see block lyrics)

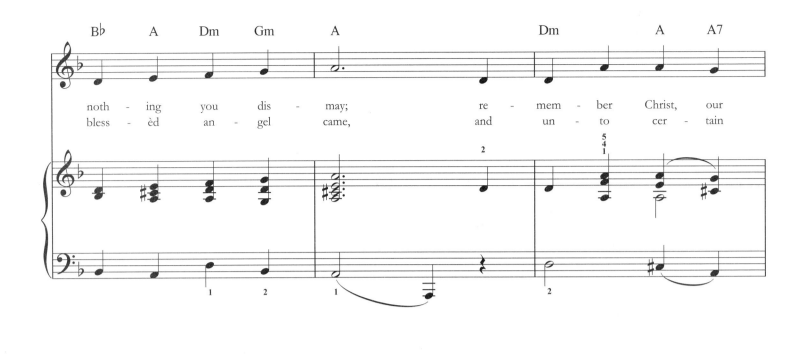

nothing you dismay; remember Christ, our
blessèd angel came, and unto certain

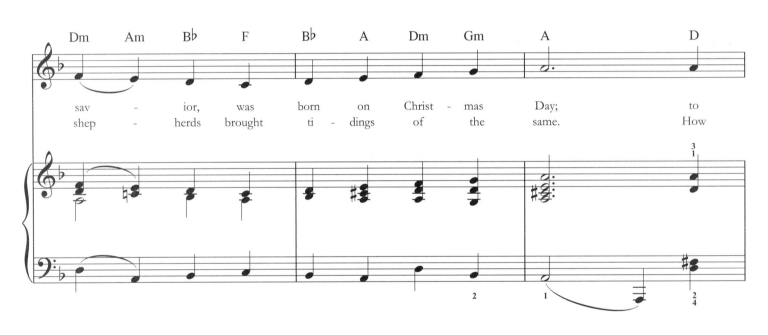

savior, was born on Christmas Day; to
shepherds brought tidings of the same. How

save us all from Satan's power when we were gone a-
that in Bethlehem was born when the Son of God by

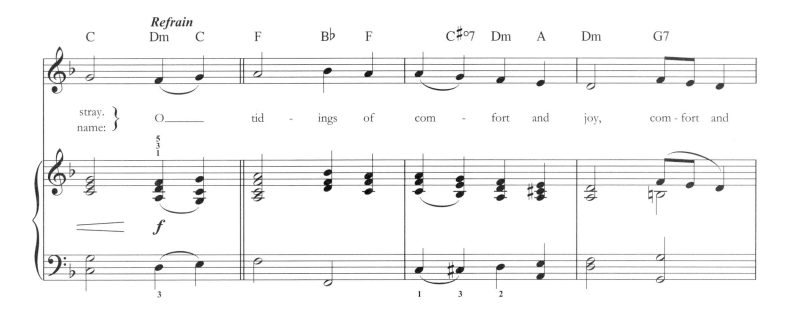

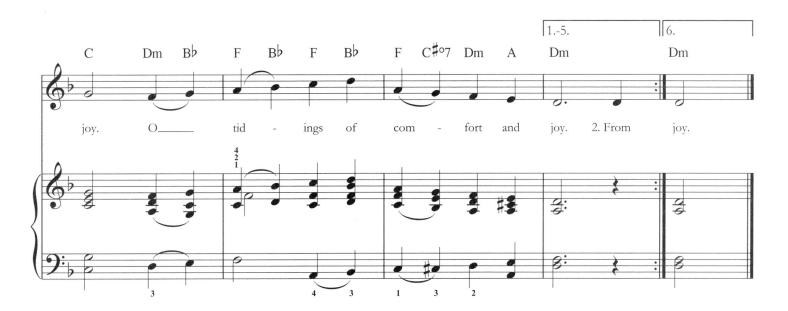

Verse 3:
"Fear not," then said the angel,
"Let nothing you affright,
This day is born a Savior
Of virtue, power and might;
So frequently to vanquish all
The friends of Satan quite:"
Refrain

Verse 4:
The shepherds at these tidings
Rejoicèd much in mind,
And left their flocks a-feeding
In tempest, storm, and wind,
And went to Bethlehem straightway
This blessèd babe to find:
Refrain

Verse 5:
And when they came to Bethlehem,
Where our sweet Savior lay,
They found him in a manger,
Where oxen feed on hay;
His mother Mary kneeling,
Unto the Lord did pray:
Refrain

Verse 6:
Now to the Lord sing praises,
All you within this place,
And with true love and brotherhood
Each other now embrace;
This holy tide of Christmas
All others doth deface:
Refrain

Go Tell It on the Mountain

Words by John W. Work, Jr.
Music: African-American Spiritual

Verse 3:
And lo, when they had seen it,
They all bowed down and prayed;
Then they travelled on together,
To where the Babe was laid.
Refrain

Verse 4:
He made me a watchman,
Upon the city wall,
And if I am a Christian,
I am the least of all.
Refrain

Good Christian Men, Rejoice

Traditional German Carol

1. Good Chris - tian men, re - joice_____ with heart, and soul, and
Chris - tian men, re - joice_____ with heart, and soul, and
(Verse 3 see block lyrics)

voice;_____ give ye heed to what we say: News! News!
voice;_____ now ye hear of end - less bliss: Joy! Joy!

Verse 3:

Good Christian men, rejoice

With heart, and soul, and voice;

Now ye need not fear the grave:

Peace! Peace! Jesus Christ was born to save!

He calls you one and calls you all

To gain His everlasting hall;

Christ was born to save!

Christ was born to save!

Good King Wenceslas

Words by John M. Neale
Music: Traditional Swedish Melody

Moderately fast
D C B7 Em D7 G C G D7 Em C G
mf
G Em Am G C D C G C D7 G
1. Good King Wen - ces - las looked out, on the Feast of Ste - phen.
2. "Hith - er, page, and stand by me, if though knowst it, tel - ling,
(Verses 3-5 see block lyrics)
Em Am G C D C G C D7 G
When the snow lay 'round a - bout, deep and crisp and e - ven.
yon - der pea - sant, who is he? Where and what his dwel - ling?"

Brightly shone the moon that night, though the frost was cruel,
when a poor man came in sight, gath-'ring winter fuel.

"Sire, he lives a good league hence underneath the mountain
right against the forest fence by Saint Agnes' fountain."

Verse 3:

"Bring me flesh and bring me wine,
Bring me pine logs hither:
Thou and I will see him dine
When we bear them thither."
Page and monarch, forth they went,
Forth they went together
Through the rude wind's wild lament
And the bitter weather.

Verse 4:

"Sire, the night is darker now,
And the wind grows stronger;
Fails my heart, I know not how,
I can go no longer."
"Mark my footsteps, good my page;
Tread thou in them boldly:
Thou shalt find the winter's rage
Freeze thy blood less coldly."

Verse 5:

In his master's steps he trod,
Where the snow lay dinted;
Heat was in the very sod,
Which the Saint had printed.
Therefore, Christian men be sure,
Wealth or rank possessing,
Ye who now will bless the poor,
Shall yourselves find blessing.

Hallelujah Chorus
from *Messiah*

By George Frideric Handel

In Dulci Jubilo

Traditional German Carol

(Verses 3 & 4 see block lyrics)

1. In dul - ci - ju - bi - lo,_____ let us our hom - age show;_____
Je - su par - vu - le! My heart is sore for thee!_____

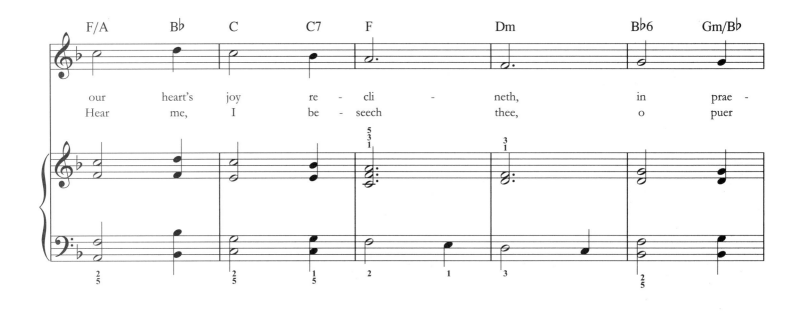

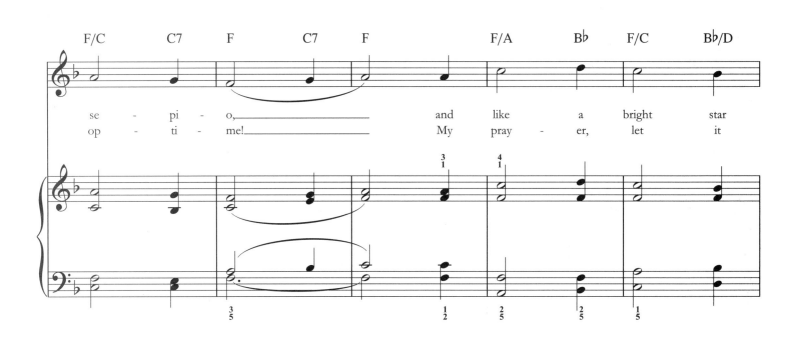

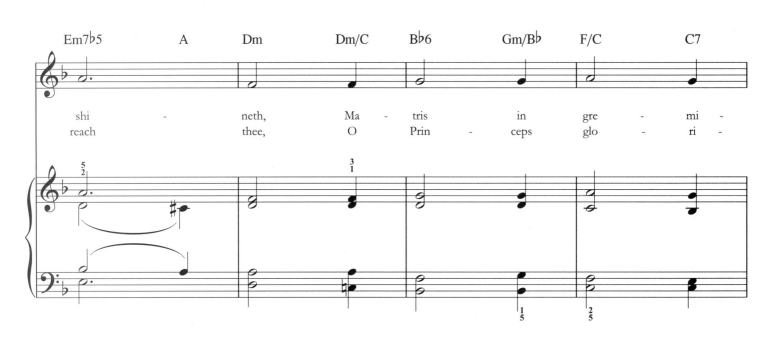

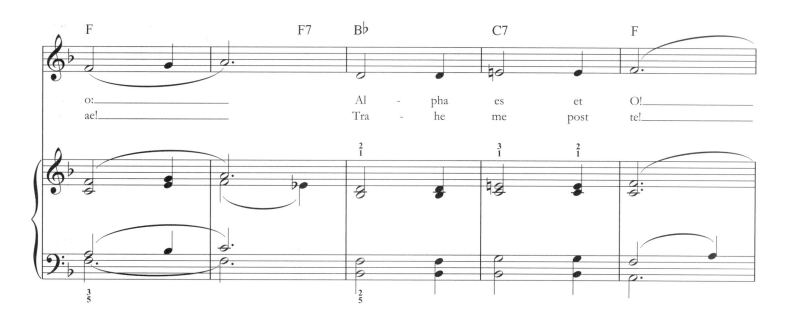

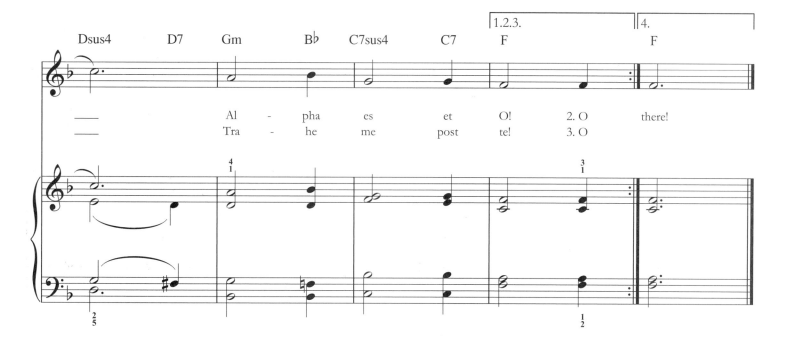

Verse 3:

O Patris caritas!
O Nati lenitas!
Deep were we stainèd,
Per nostra crimina;
But thou has for us gainèd,
Coelorum gaudia:
O that we were there!
O that we were there!

Verse 4:

Ubi sunt gaudia, where,
If that they be not there?
There, are angels singing,
Nova cantica;
There the bells are ringing,
In Regis curia:
O that we were there!
O that we were there!

Hark! The Herald Angels Sing

Words by Charles Wesley
Music by Felix Mendelssohn

Joyfully

1. Hark! The her - ald an - gels sing:___ "Glo - ry to the new - born King!
2. Christ, by high - est heaven a - dored,___ Christ, the e - ver - las - ting Lord;
(Verse 3 see block lyrics)

Peace on earth and mer - cy mild,___ God and sin - ners rec - on - ciled!"
Late in time be - hold him come,___ off - spring of a Vir - gin's womb.

Verse 3:

Hail the heaven-born Prince of Peace!

Hail the Son of Righteousness!

Light and life to all He brings,

Risen with healing in His wings.

Mild He lays His glory by,

Born that man no more may die,

Born to raise the sons of earth,

Born to give them second birth.

Refrain

The Holly and the Ivy

Traditional English Carol

1. The hol - ly and the i - vy, when they are both full grown, of____
hol - ly bears a blos - som as white as the flow'r, and____

(Verses 3-6 see block lyrics)

all the trees that are in the wood, the____ hol - ly bears the crown.
Mar - y bore sweet Je - sus Christ to____ be our sweet sa - vior. The

ris-ing of the sun_____ and the run-ning of the deer, the_____

play-ing of the mer-ry or-gan, sweet sing-ing in the choir. 2. The choir.

Verse 3:
The holly bears a berry
A red as any blood,
And Mary bore sweet Jesus Christ
To do poor sinners good.
Refrain

Verse 4:
The holly bears a prickle
As sharp as any thorn,
And Mary bore sweet Jesus Christ
On Christmas Day in the morn.
Refrain

Verse 5:
The holly bears a bark
A bitter as any gall,
And Mary bore sweet Jesus Christ
For to redeem us all.
Refrain

Verse 6:
The holly and the ivy,
When they are both full grown,
Of all the trees that are in the wood,
The holly bears the crown.
Refrain

I Saw Three Ships

Traditional English Carol

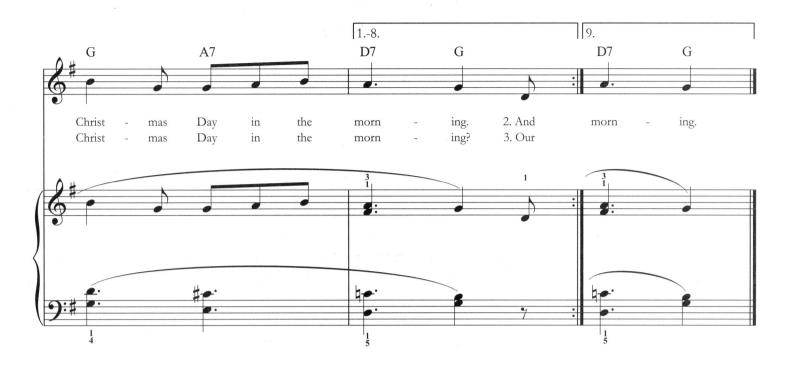

Verse 3:
Our Savior Christ and his lady,
On Christmas Day, on Christmas Day,
Our Savior Christ and his lady,
On Christmas Day in the morning.

Verse 4:
Pray, whither sailed those ships all three?
On Christmas Day, on Christmas Day,
Pray, whither sailed those ships all three?
On Christmas Day in the morning.

Verse 5:
O, they sailed into Bethlehem,
On Christmas Day, on Christmas Day,
O, they sailed into Bethlehem,
On Christmas Day in the morning.

Verse 6:
And all the bells on earth shall ring,
On Christmas Day, on Christmas Day,
And all the bells on earth shall ring,
On Christmas Day in the morning.

Verse 7:
And all the angels in heaven shall sing,
On Christmas Day, on Christmas Day,
And all the angels in heaven shall sing,
On Christmas Day in the morning.

Verse 8:
And all the souls on earth shall sing,
On Christmas Day, on Christmas Day,
And all the souls on earth shall sing,
On Christmas Day in the morning.

Verse 9:
Then let us all rejoice amen!
On Christmas Day, on Christmas Day,
Then let us all rejoice amen!
On Christmas Day in the morning.

In the Bleak Midwinter

Words by Christina Rossetti

Music by Gustav Holst

Verse 3:

Enough for him, whom cherubim
Worship night and day,
A breastful of milk
And a manger full of hay.
Enough for him, whom angels
Fall down before,
The ox and ass and camel,
Which adore.

Verse 4:

Angels and archangels
May have gathered there;
Cherubim and seraphim
Filled the air.
But his mother, Mary,
In her maiden bliss,
Worshipped the Messiah
Worshipped with a kiss.

Verse 5:

What can I give him,
Poor as I am?
If I were a shepherd,
I would bring a lamb.
If I were a wise man,
I would do my part.
What I can I give him,
Jesus, take my heart.

It Came Upon the Midnight Clear

Words by Edmund H. Sears
Music by Richard S. Willis

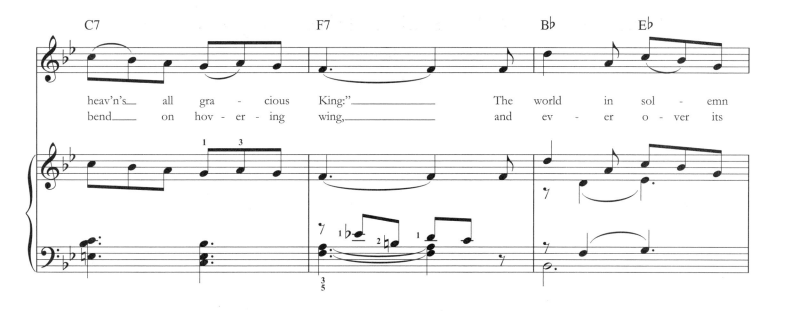

heav'n's all gra - cious King:"_____ The world in sol - emn
bend____ on hov - er - ing wing,_____ and ev - er o - ver its

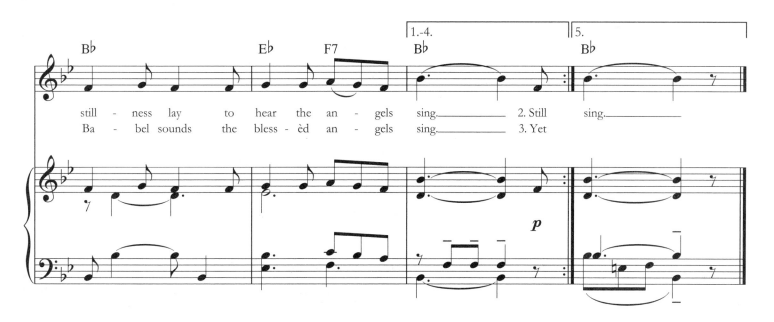

still - ness lay to hear the an - gels sing._____ 2. Still sing.____
Ba - bel sounds the bless - èd an - gels sing._____ 3. Yet

Verse 3:

Yet with the woes of sin and strife
The world has suffered long;
Beneath the angel-strain have rolled
Two thousand years of wrong;
And man, at war with man, hears not
The love song, which they bring.
O hush the noise, ye men of strife,
And hear the angels sing.

Verse 4:

And ye, beneath life's crushing load,
Whose forms are bending low,
Who toil along the climbing way
With painful steps and slow:
Look now for glad and golden hours
Come swiftly on the wing;
O rest beside the weary road
And hear the angels sing.

Verse 5:

For lo! the days are hastening on,
By prophet bards foretold,
When with the ever-circling years
Comes 'round the Age of Gold.
When peace shall over all the earth
Its ancient splendors fling,
And the whole world give back the song,
Which now the angels sing.

Jesu, Joy of Man's Desiring
from *Cantata 147*

By Johann Sebastian Bach

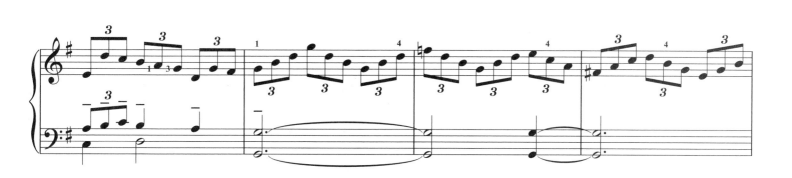

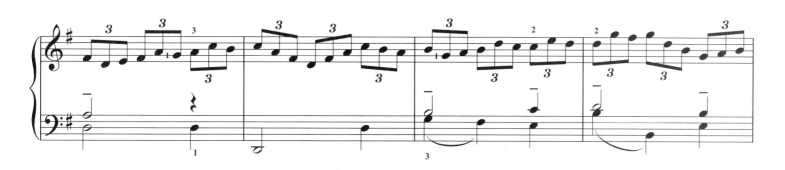

rall. poco a poco

Jingle Bells

By James S. Pierpont

1. We're dash - ing through the snow, in a
day or two a - go, I

one - horse o - pen sleigh, a - cross the fields we
thought I'd take a ride, and soon Miss Fan - nie

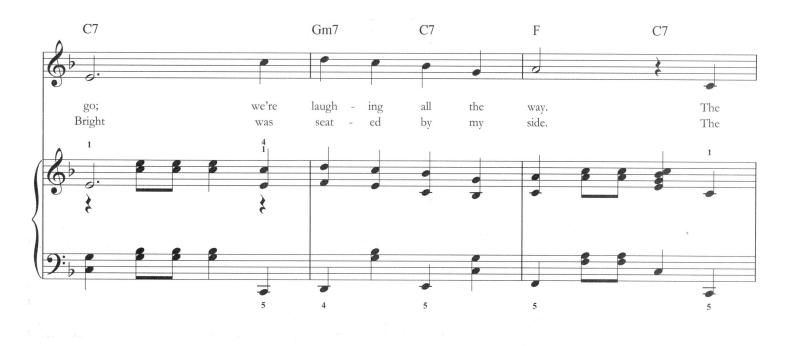

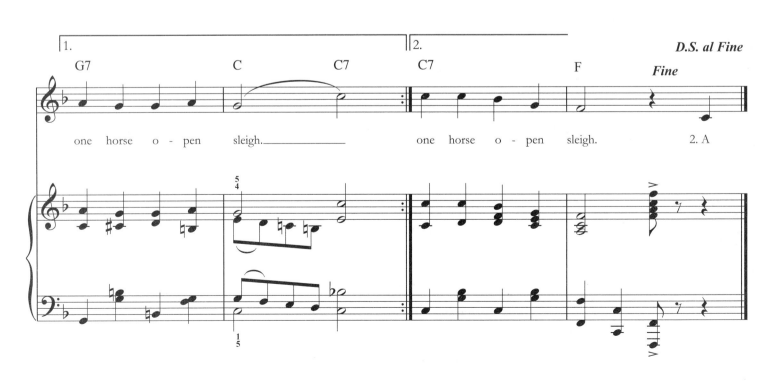

Joseph Dearest, Joseph Mild

Traditional German Carol

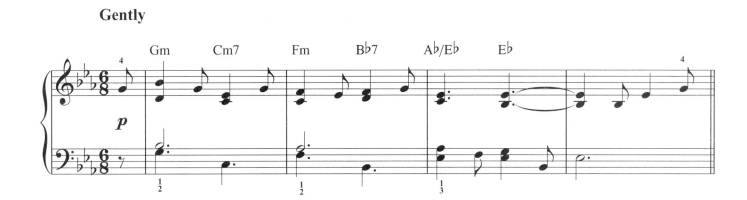

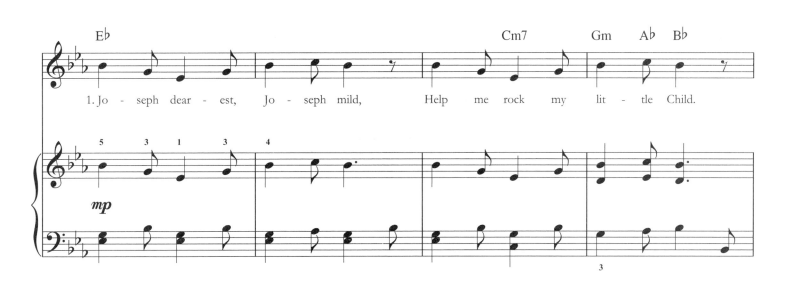

1. Jo - seph dear - est, Jo - seph mild, Help me rock my lit - tle Child.

God will give you your re - ward in heav'n a - bove, the Son of Vir - gin

Joy to the World

Words by Isaac Watts
Music by Lowell Mason

1. Joy to the world! The Lord is come; let
2. Joy to the world! The Sav - ior reigns; let

(Verse 3 see block lyrics)

earth re - ceive her King._____ Let
men their songs em - ploy;_____ while

Verse 3:

He rules the world with truth and grace,

And makes the nations prove

The glories of His righteousness,

And wonders of His love,

And wonders of His love,

And wonders, wonders of His love.

Lo! How a Rose E'er Blooming

Traditional German Carol

1. Lo, how a rose e'er bloom - ing, from
2. Lo, how a rose came spring - ing, I -

ten - der root___ has sprung. To all the
sa - iah did___ pro - claim; while all the

world be-stow - ing what men of old_____ have sung.
heav'ns were sing - ing the rose by Mar - y came.

There bloomed a love-ly flow'r though win-ter's
Through God's al - might-y pow'r the world sal -

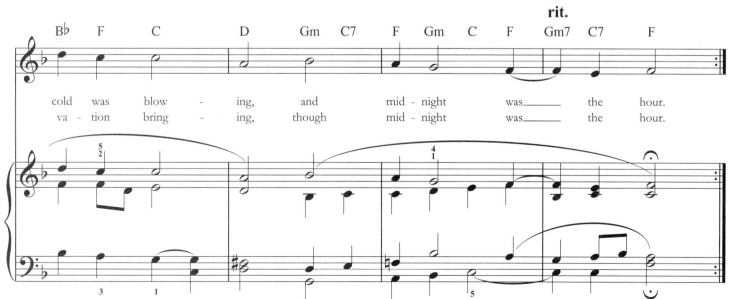

cold was blow - ing, and mid-night was_____ the hour.
va - tion bring - ing, though mid-night was_____ the hour.

83

March of the Kings

Traditional Provençal Carol

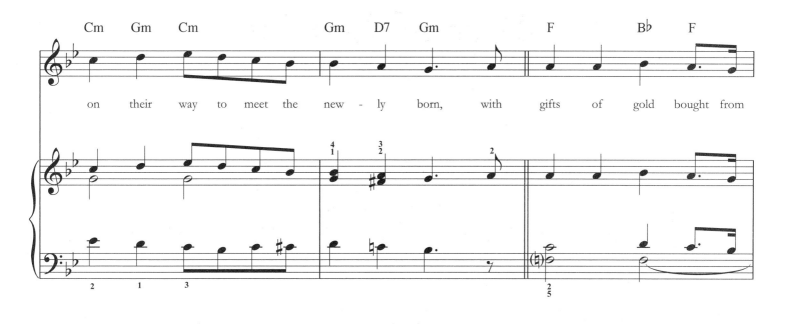

on their way to meet the new - ly born, with gifts of gold bought from

far a - way and val - iant war - riors to guard the ro - yal trea - sure; with

gifts of gold bought from far a - way, their shields all shin - ing in their bright ar - ray.

O Christmas Tree

Traditional German Carol

Moderately

1. O Christ - mas Tree, O Christ - mas Tree, thy
Christ - mas Tree, O Christ - mas Tree, you

leaves are so un - chang - ing. O Christ - mas Tree, O
fill our hearts with gaie - ty. O Christ - mas Tree, O

Christ - mas Tree, thy leaves are so un -
Christ - mas Tree, you fill our hearts with

chang - ing. Not on - ly green when
gaie - ty. On Christ - mas Day you

sum - mer's here, but al - so when 'tis
stand so tall, af - ford - ing joy to

cold and drear. O Christ - mas Tree, O
one and all. O Christ - mas Tree, O

Christ - mas Tree, thy leaves are so un -
Christ - mas Tree, you fill our hearts with

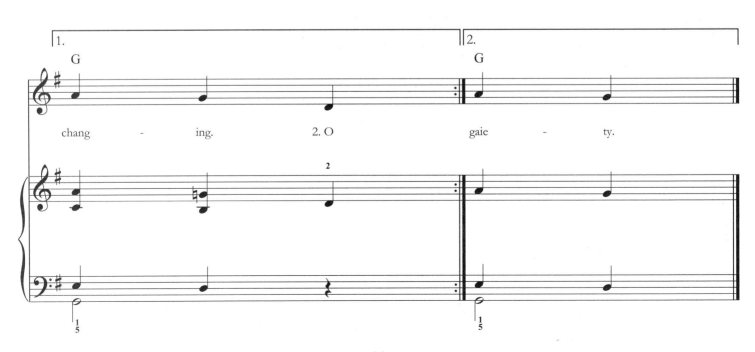

1.
chang - ing. 2. O

2.
gaie - ty.

O Come, O Come Emmanuel

Traditional French Carol

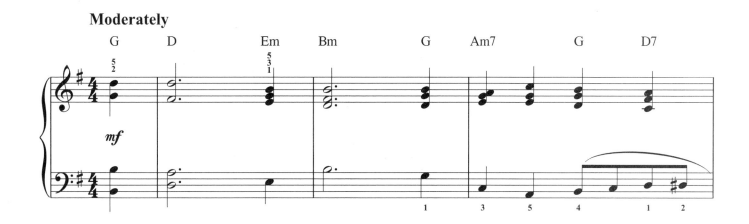

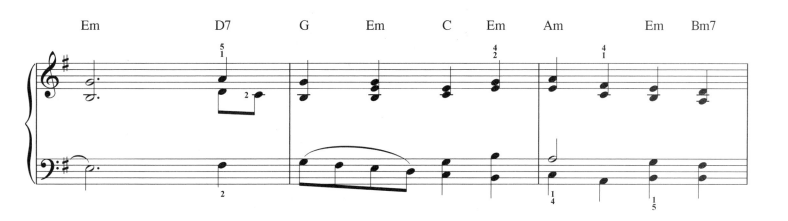

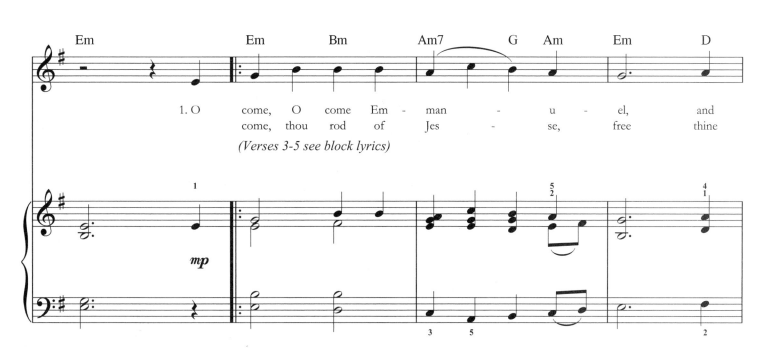

1. O come, O come Em - man - u - el, and
come, thou rod of Jes - se, free and thine

(Verses 3-5 see block lyrics)

ran - som cap - tive Is - ra - el, that
own from Sa - tan's tyr - an - ny; that from

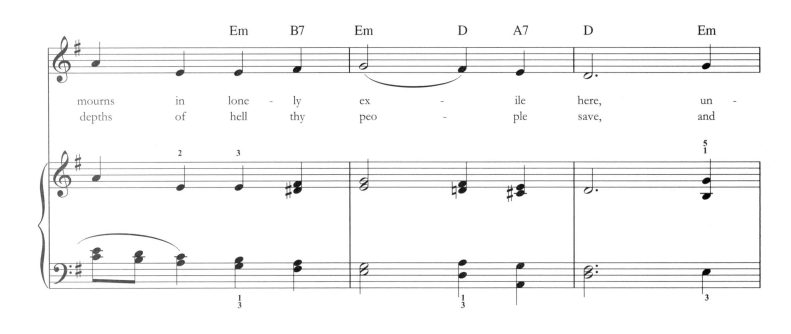

mourns in lone - ly ex - ile here, un -
depths of hell thy peo - ple save, and

Refrain

til the Son of God_____ ap - pear. } Re -
give them vict - 'ry o'er_____ the grave. }

f

90

joice! Re - joice! Em - man - u - el shall

come to thee, O Is - ra - el. 2. O el.

Verse 3:
O come, Thou day spring, come and cheer
Our spirits by Thine advent here;
Disperse the gloomy clouds of night,
And death's dark shadows put to flight.
Refrain

Verse 4:
O come, O come thou Lord of might,
Who to thy tribes, on Sinai's height,
In ancient times didst give the law
In cloud, and majesty, and awe.
Refrain

Verse 5:
O come, thou key of David, come,
And span wide our heavenly home;
Make safe the way that leads on high,
And close the path to misery.
Refrain

O Come, All Ye Faithful

Words by John F. Wade

Music: Traditional

hem. Come and be - hold him, born the King of an - gels: } O
bove! Glo - ry to God, all glo - ry in the high - est: } O

come, let us a - dore him. O come, let us a - dore him. O

come, let us a - dore him,___ Christ____ the Lord. Lord.

Verse 3:

Yea, Lord, we greet Thee, born this happy morning,

Jesus, to Thee be all glory giv'n;

Word of the Father, now in the flesh appearing:

Refrain

93

O Come, Little Children

Words by Christoph von Schmid
Music by Johann A. P. Schulz

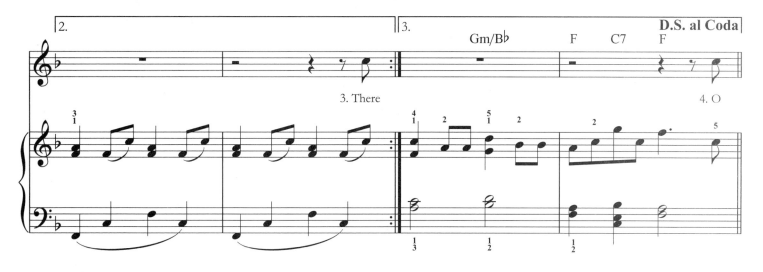

Verse 3:

There lies sleeping Jesus on hay and on straw.
Before Him the shepherds are kneeling in awe.
Above Him the angels in jubilance sing,
While Mary and Joseph keep watch on the King.

Verse 4:

O kneel with the shepherds and worship the King
Give thanks to our God for the love that He brings.
Enjoy, holy children, your glad voices raised,
And join with the angels in jubilant praise.

O Holy Night

By Adolphe Adam

peared and the soul felt His worth._____ A thrill of hope, the
wise men__ from the O - rient land._____ The King of Kings lay

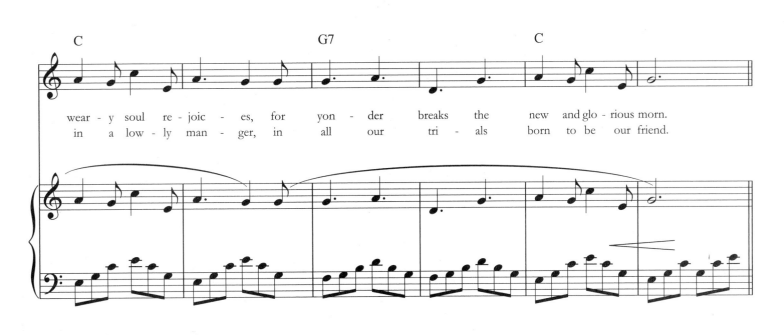

wear - y soul re - joic - es, for yon - der breaks the new and glo - rious morn.
in a low - ly man - ger, in all our tri - als born to be our friend.

Fall_____ on your knees,_____ O hear_____ the an - gel
He_____ knows our need,_____ to our_____ weak - ness no

Verse 3:

Truly He taught us to love one another;

His law is love, and His gospel is peace.

Chains shall He break, for the slave is our brother,

And in His name all oppression shall cease.

Sweet hymns of joy in grateful chorus rise we,

Let all within us praise His holy name.

Christ is the Lord,

Then ever, ever praise we;

His pow'r and glory ever more proclaim,

His pow'r and glory ever more proclaim.

The Virgin's Slumber Song

Words by Edward Teschemacher
Music by Max Reger

And soft and sweet - ly sings a bird___ up - on the bough:

Ah, ba - by, dear___ one,

slum - ber now!

Happy is Thy laugh - ter, ho - ly is___ Thy

O Little Town of Bethlehem

Words by Phillips Brooks
Music by Lewis H. Redner

shin — eth the ev — er — last — ing light: The hopes and fears of
geth — er pro — claim the ho — ly birth! And prais — es sing to

all the years are met in thee to — night. 2. For el.
God the King, and peace to men on earth! 3. How

Verse 3:
How silently, how silently
The wondrous gift is giv'n!
So God imparts to human hearts
The blessings of His heav'n.
No ear may hear His coming,
But in this world of sin,
Where meek souls will receive Him still
The dear Christ enters in.

Verse 4:
O Holy Child of Bethlehem!
Descend to us, we pray;
Cast out our sin, and enter in;
Be born in us today.
We hear the Christmas angels,
The great glad tidings tell;
O come to us, abide with us,
Our Lord Emmanuel.

O Sanctissima

Traditional

With spirited motion

1. Oh, how joy - ful - ly,_____ oh, how mer - ri - ly_____
2. Oh, how joy - ful - ly,_____ oh, how mer - ri - ly_____

(Verse 3 see block lyrics)

Christ - mas comes with its grace di - vine!
Christ - mas comes with its grace di - vine!

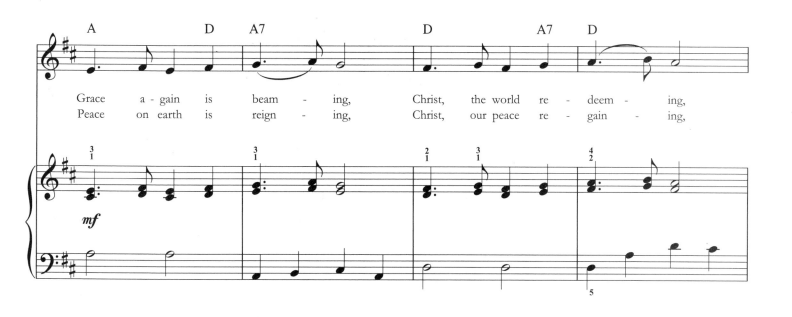

Grace a - gain is beam - ing, Christ, the world re - deem - ing,
Peace on earth is reign - ing, Christ, our peace re - gain - ing,

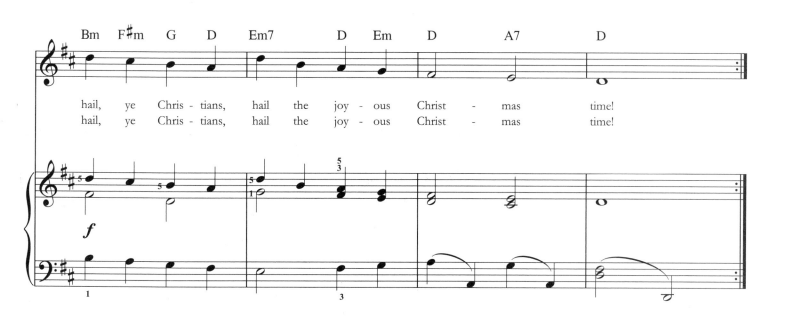

hail, ye Chris - tians, hail the joy - ous Christ - mas time!
hail, ye Chris - tians, hail the joy - ous Christ - mas time!

Verse 3:

Oh, how joyfully,

Oh, how merrily

Christmas comes with its life divine!

Angels high in glory

Chant the Christmas story,

Hail, ye Christians,

Hail the joyous Christmas time!

Once in Royal David's City

Words by Cecil F. Alexander
Music by Henry J. Gauntlett

1. Once in roy - al Da - vid's city stood a low - ly
2. He came down to earth from heav - en, who is God and

(Verses 3-6 see block lyrics)

cat - tle shed, where a moth - er laid her ba - by
Lord of all, and His shel - ter was a sta - ble,

Verse 3:

And, through all His wondrous Childhood,
He would honor and obey,
Love and watch the lowly Maiden
In whose gentle arms He lay.
Christian children all must be
Mild, obedient, good as He.

Verse 4:

For He is our childhood's pattern,
Day by day like us He grew.
He was little, weak, and helpless;
Tears and smiles like us He knew.
And He feeleth for our sadness,
And He shareth in our gladness.

Verse 5:

And our eyes at last shall see Him
Through His own redeeming love.
For that Child so dear and gentle
Is our Lord in heaven above.
And He leads His children on
To the place where He is gone.

Verse 6:

Not in that poor lowly stable
With the oxen standing by,
We shall see Him, but in Heaven,
Set at God's right hand on high.
When like stars His children crown'd,
All in white shall wait around.

Panis Angelicus

By César Franck

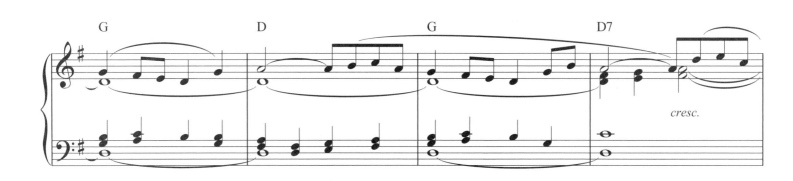

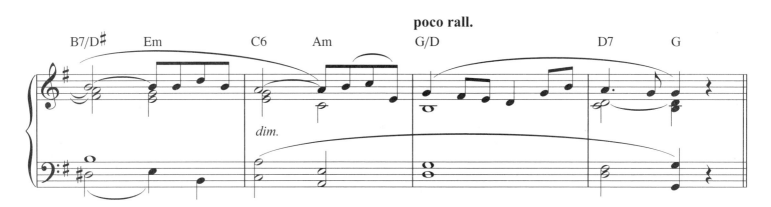

Pat-A-Pan

Traditional French Carol

1. Wil - lie, take your lit - tle drum; Ro - bin take your
men of old - en days, to the King of
(Verse 3 see block lyrics)

flute and come; let us hear the mu - sic
kings and gave praise, on their in - stru - ments they

Verse 3:

God and man this day become
Joined as one with flute and drum,
When we hear the music play,
Tu-re-lu-re-lu,
Pat-a-pat-a-pan,
When we hear the music play,
On this joyful Christmas Day!

Silent Night

Words by Josef Mohr
Music by Franz Gruber

1. Si - lent night! Ho - ly night! All is
2. Si - lent night! Ho - ly night! Shep - herds

(Verse 3 see block lyrics)

calm, all is bright. 'round yon Vir - gin
quake at the sight! Glo - ries stream from

Verse 3:

Silent night! Holy night!
Son of God, love's pure light,
Radiant beams from Thy holy face,
With the dawn of redeeming grace.
Jesus, Lord, at Thy birth.
Jesus, Lord, at Thy birth.

The Skater's Waltz

By Emil Waldteufel

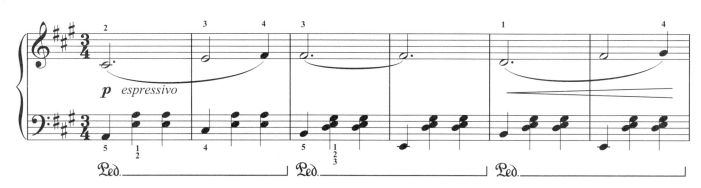

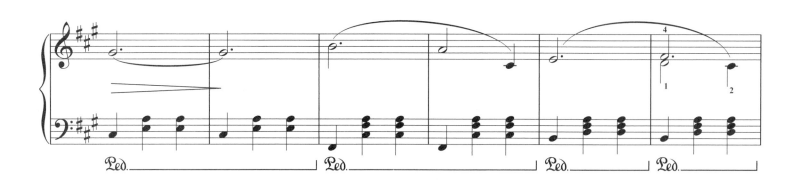

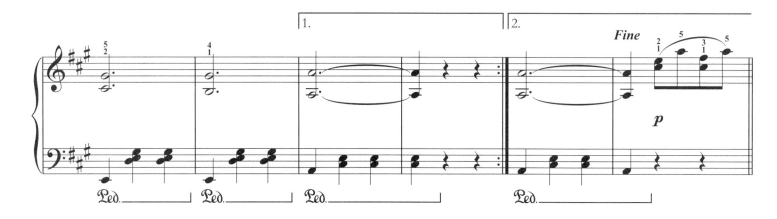

The Sleigh Ride

Leopold Mozart

Lively ♩ = 104

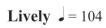

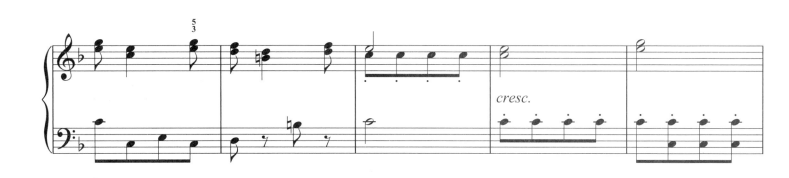

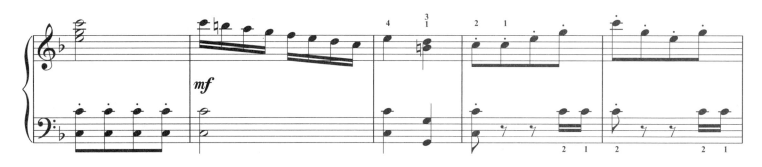

Toyland

from *Babes in Toyland*

By Victor Herbert

Moderately slow

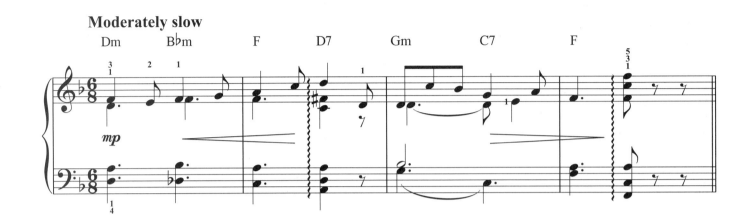

a tempo

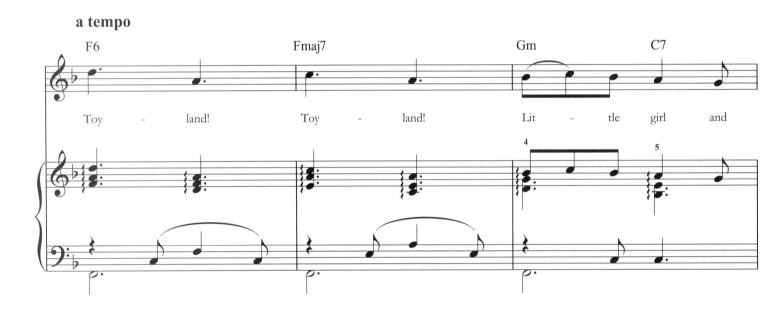

Toy - land! Toy - land! Lit - tle girl and

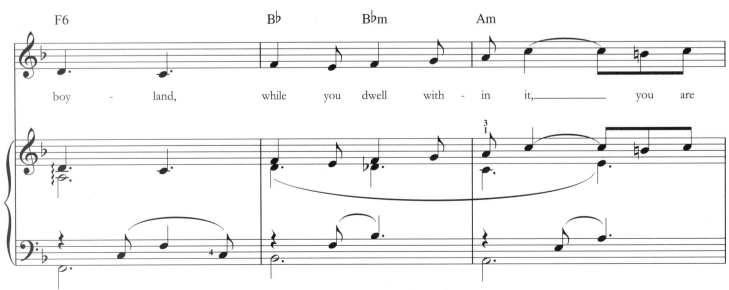

boy - land, while you dwell with - in it,_____ you are

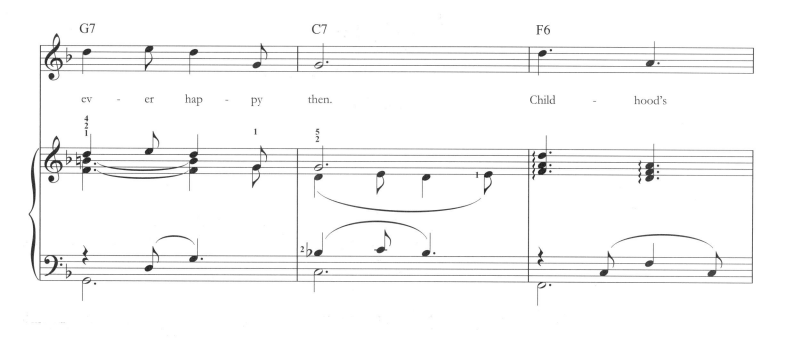

The Twelve Days of Christmas

Traditional English Carol

Two tur - tle doves, and a par - tridge__ in a pear tree. 5. On the fifth day of Christ - mas my

true love sent to me: Five gold__ rings, Four__ call - ing birds, Three French hens,

Two__ tur - tle doves, and a par - tridge__ in a pear tree.

6. On the
7. On the
8. On the
9. On the
10. On the
11. On the
12. On the

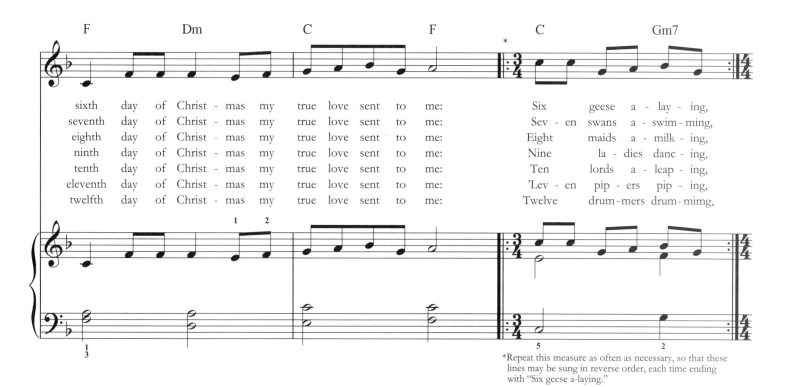

sixth day of Christ-mas my true love sent to me: Six geese a-lay-ing,
seventh day of Christ-mas my true love sent to me: Sev-en swans a-swim-ming,
eighth day of Christ-mas my true love sent to me: Eight maids a-milk-ing,
ninth day of Christ-mas my true love sent to me: Nine la-dies danc-ing,
tenth day of Christ-mas my true love sent to me: Ten lords a-leap-ing,
eleventh day of Christ-mas my true love sent to me: 'Lev-en pip-ers pip-ing,
twelfth day of Christ-mas my true love sent to me: Twelve drum-mers drum-mimg,

*Repeat this measure as often as necessary, so that these
lines may be sung in reverse order, each time ending
with "Six geese a-laying."

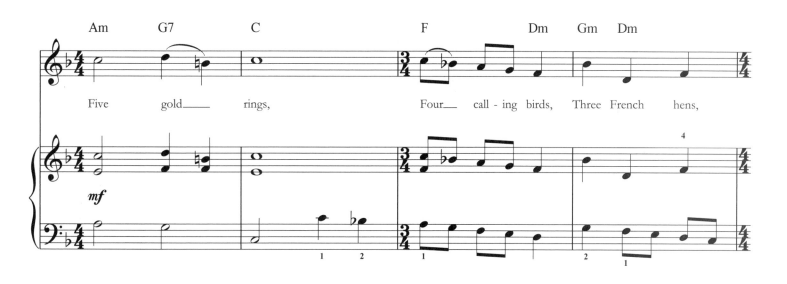

Five gold___ rings, Four__ call-ing birds, Three French hens,

Two__ tur-tle doves, and a par-tridge__ in a pear tree. tree.

We Three Kings of Orient Are

By John H. Hopkins

With spirit

1. We three kings of o-ri-ent are, bear-ing gifts we
2. Born a King on Beth-le-hem plain. Gold I bring to

(Verses 3-5 see block lyrics)

trav-erse a-far, field and foun-tain, moor and moun-tain,
crown Him a-gain. King for-ev-er, ceas-ing nev-er;

Verse 3:

Frankincense to offer have I;
Incense owns a Deity nigh.
Prayer and praising, all men raising
Worship Him, God most high.
Refrain

Verse 4:

Myrrh is mine; its bitter perfume
Breathes a life of gathering gloom.
Sorrowing, sighing, bleeding, dying,
Sealed in the stone cold tomb.
Refrain

Verse 5:

Glorious now behold Him arise,
King and God and sacrifice.
Heaven sings Alleluia;
Alleluia the earth replies.
Refrain

129

We Wish You a Merry Christmas

Traditional English Carol

Verse 3:
We won't go until we got some,
We won't go until we got some,
We won't go until we got some,
So bring some out here!
Refrain

What Child Is This?

Words by William C. Dix

Verse 3:
So bring Him incense, gold, and myrrh,
Come peasant, king, to own Him.
The King of Kings salvation brings,
Let loving hearts enthrone Him.
Refrain

133

The Wassail Song

Traditional English Carol

Moderately fast, with spirit

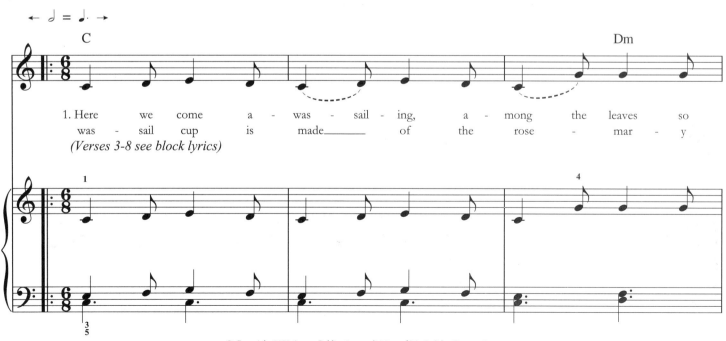

1. Here we come a-was-sail-ing, a-mong the leaves so
was-sail cup is made____ of the rose-mar-y

(Verses 3-8 see block lyrics)

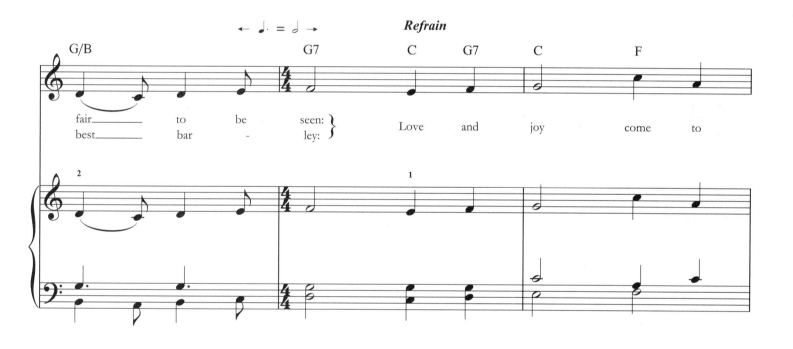

Verse 3:
We are not daily beggars
That go from door to door,
But we are neighbors' children
That 'round the table go:
Refrain

Verse 4:
Call up the butler of this house;
Put on his golden ring.
Let him bring us up a glass of beer,
And better we shall sing:
Refrain

Verse 5:
We have a little purse
Of stretching leather skin;
We want a little money
To line it well within:
Refrain

Verse 6:
Bring us out a table,
And spread it with a cloth;
Bring us out a mouldy cheese,
And some of your Christmas loaf:
Refrain

Verse 7:
God bless the master of this house,
Likewise the mistress too;
And all the little children
That 'round the table go:
Refrain

Verse 8:
Good master and good mistress
While you're sitting by the fire,
Pray think of us poor children
Who wonder in the mire:
Refrain